CIRQUE DU SOLEIL®

The Spark

CIRQUE DU SOLEIL®

Igniting the Creative Fire

The Spark

That Lives Within Us All

Created by Lyn Heward
and written by John U. Bacon

CURRENCY

DOUBLEDAY

NEW YORK LONDON TORONTO SYDNEY AUCKLAND

A CURRENCY BOOK
PUBLISHED BY DOUBLEDAY
a division of Random House, Inc.

CURRENCY is a trademark of Random House, Inc., and DOUBLEDAY is a registered trademark of Random House, Inc.

Cataloging-in-Publication Data is on file with the Library of Congress.

ISBN 0-385-51651-7

Book design by Chris Welch

PRINTED IN THE UNITED STATES OF AMERICA

SPECIAL SALES
Currency Books are available at special discounts for bulk purchases for sales promotions or premiums. Special editions, including personalized covers, excerpts of existing books, and corporate imprints, can be created in large quantities for special needs. For more information, write to Special Markets, Currency Books, specialmarkets@randomhouse.com.

1 3 5 7 9 10 8 6 4 2

FIRST EDITION

*To Guy and the multitude of artists, artisans,
technicians, employees, and managers of Cirque du Soleil
who live each day creatively and in so doing
have inspired me immeasurably.*

—Lyn

Foreword

By Guy Laliberté, Founder and CEO

The Spark is not only a whirlwind tour of Cirque du Soleil's operations and activities, it is above all an intimate encounter with its employees who live each day creatively. And, although it tells the tale of one man's voyage of self-discovery, *The Spark* unveils a variety of simple ways by which anyone can become more creative, see greater possibilities, and create his or her own vision for the future.

With more than 3,000 full-time employees, artists, artisans, technicians, and managers around the world, it would be impossible to recognize each and every creative contribution individually; therefore many of the unique characters in this book are composites of the generous, passionate, and talented men and women who have shared the Cirque du Soleil experience. Their stories, however, are real. From their great expectations and "magnificent dreams," creative products have emerged. They have learned to surrender to their senses, trust their instincts, take risks, and meet new challenges in an artistic and nurturing environment. They work alone and they work together learning to connect with and touch people in new ways, endeavouring always to reinvent themselves. And they aspire to give back to the world in the endless continuum of change, exchange, and renewal; they are catalysts.

From a tiny spark a great fire was kindled and its flames warmed the world . . .

chapter one

Through the White Doors

If You Have No Idea What You're Looking For . . .

When people ask where my remarkable journey began, I tell them it was somewhere between the first and seventh doors. At least, that's where I found myself after I left behind the cacophony of the casino, with its blinking lights, rolling dice, and excitement around every corner. As fascinated as I was with the land of chance, I needed to give my senses a brief respite from the spinning wheels of fortune.

I was searching for something, though for what, I didn't know. Something extraordinary. Something beyond the mundane world of marketing and money that had brought me to Las Vegas in the first place. Something beyond the grind that had become my life. Of course, if you have no idea what you're looking for, it's pretty hard to find it.

I was about to escape to my hotel room for a moment of tranquillity, when I saw two men dressed in black work outfits walking away from the slot machines toward a quieter part of the casino. It was in an almost dreamlike state that I followed them. They disappeared through a plain white door—perhaps the only portal in the casino that didn't seem to announce what was on the other side. Intrigued, I pushed on it, and it opened, leading me into a completely silent, perfectly white corridor, lit so well it almost glowed with energy. A few feet in front of me was another door, just as pristine, every bit as beckoning. I opened it, though more tentatively than the first, for while I could surely pass off wandering through one wrong door as a mistake, opening the second seemed a more serious offense.

Behind the second white door was a third. Who were those men and where were they going? And what would I do when I found them? What kind of Alice-down-the-rabbit-hole adventure was I getting myself into? As I passed through the next door, I noticed a security camera above and a security desk to my left, and I felt my shoulders tense up. What were they trying to protect here? But there was not a soul in sight, so I kept going. By the time I reached the sixth door, I had accepted that I had no idea where the corridor was leading me—but I had the unmistakable sense that, as each door closed behind me, I was one step closer to what I was searching for.

As I pushed through the seventh door, I realized I had reached the end of the corridor and the beginning of my journey. The final door opened into a vast theatre. Rows of plush blue seats arced to my left. The ceiling soared a hundred feet above me, and I resisted the urge to call out and hear the sound of my voice echoing, if only to prove to myself that I wasn't dreaming.

To my right was the strangest stage I'd ever encountered. I watched as a mysterious monolithic structure, maybe forty by eighty feet, moved left and right, forward and back, and finally stood straight up and down, as if defying gravity. I couldn't determine its purpose—surely it wasn't part of the stage? You'd have to be Spiderman to scale such a precipice!

On the other side of the theatre, I could see the men who'd unwittingly led me through the doors. They were tinkering with equipment on the revolving column, which was perched precariously behind a stage floor that opened into a seemingly bottomless abyss. Though they were a good twenty yards away, I could hear their voices; the acoustics of the theatre were that crisp. I could detect several distinct accents among the half-dozen people around the stage—Scottish, Russian, Texan, and French Canadian.

They were so focused on their work that no one seemed to notice I was there. My curiosity was aroused in a way it hadn't been since college, when every experience was a new adventure and I didn't have to worry about the consequences of my actions the way I did now; my mind seemed alive to the possibilities my surroundings presented. I sat down in one of the theatre seats, in the middle of everything, and took it all in.

The enormous theatre was less a stage than a cavernous aviary, framed by huge catwalks constructed of aged wooden planks and copper railing, an intriguing contrast to the ultramodern style of the MGM Grand Hotel. It possessed a timeless quality, as if I'd stepped foot in an edifice that had been built long before Las Vegas existed.

I might have sat there for ten or twenty minutes, just watching and listening.

Eventually, someone noticed me: a friendly-looking woman who seemed to appear out of nowhere—slender, middle-aged, with short, dark red hair and a stylish suede jacket. She made her way along a row of seats toward me. While I was no doubt somewhere I shouldn't be, she seemed more curious about my presence than upset.

Normally, I would have apologized profusely for trespassing, and jumped up to leave. But something held me back.

"Hello, there," she said when she was only a couple of rows away.

"Hello," I said with a small nod. I assumed I was going to get kicked out; I didn't see any point in attempting to fight it. But instead of asking me to leave, the woman offered her hand.

"I'm Diane," she said.

"And I'm Frank," I responded. She settled in a couple seats to my right, taking in the scene before us. Had she fallen into this alternative universe the same way I had?

"Pretty breathtaking, isn't it?" she asked, gesturing outward with her hand.

"I've never seen anything like it before," I said.

"I like to think of it as a theatre of unfulfilled dreams and great expectations."

I didn't know quite how to respond to that. "It's so quiet, despite its size."

"Hmm," she agreed. "It can be such a soothing, tranquil place during the day. But there's a latent electricity in the air, too, don't you think? Before the shows begin, I often feel a kinetic energy in the theatre, as if it were on the verge of exploding."

No sooner had the words left her mouth than a fireball exploded above the pit in the middle of the stage; the smoke hovered for a few seconds before dissipating into the air.

"Just testing, Diane!" one of the men in black called out.

"What *is* this?" I asked. By this time I realized she belonged here, and I had certainly given myself away as an interloper. But my social graces had deserted me, leaving behind simply a sincere desire to learn more.

She laughed. "How *did* you get in here?"

I smiled, as I traced my steps back in my mind. This was no dream, I realized. I was undeniably, completely awake. "I was looking to escape a convention seminar," I explained, "and started wandering through the casino. I saw those guys," I pointed toward the riggers, "and I thought they seemed to know more about where they were going than I did, so I followed them."

"Well, I admire your sense of adventure," Diane said. "What kind of work do you do that brings you to Las Vegas?"

"I'm a sports agent," I said, somewhat apologetically.

"You don't sound overly thrilled about that."

"At first I loved it. Working with the athletes—the talent, as we call them—was exciting. I was jetting off to cities all over the country, searching for the next NBA all-star, NFL quarterback, baseball Hall of Famer." I paused, then confessed, "But somewhere along the line, my work started feeling less like a calling and more like a plain old job."

I was surprised at my candor. Why was I so willing to reveal my feelings to a stranger? I wondered. It was so unlike me—a man who made his living playing his cards close to his chest.

Diane nodded sympathetically. "Not many people seem excited by their jobs, do they?"

"No, I suppose not," I said. Off the top of my head, I really couldn't think of anyone I knew who was passionate about their work.

"What was your seminar about?"

"'Marketing Creatively,'" I said, reciting the title. "But it really wasn't about creativity. It was just about finding even more ways to make money through endorsements." When had I become so cynical about my job? "So, what *is* the show you're rehearsing? This theatre looks like a set for an Indiana Jones movie."

"You're serious?" Diane asked. "You really don't know what the show is?"

I shook my head. Instead of appearing insulted, however, Diane smiled, amused. I'm sure she was wondering who this stranger was who managed to slip through security and plop down in the middle of their theatre in the middle of the day. She shifted her shoulders toward me before speaking. "It's a show called KÀ. Have you heard of Cirque du Soleil?"

"Of course!" I said, feeling the fuzzy grasp of my surroundings finally coming into focus. "I've seen your billboards all over Las Vegas. But I'll be honest: I'm not really sure what you do."

"Well," Diane said, warming to the challenge of educating me, fishing for an introductory speech she probably hadn't had to give in years, "we're a creative entertainment company; we develop shows built around the dreams, talents, and passions of our artists and creators. Cirque was formed in Quebec in 1984, and we now have eleven shows around the world, four right here in Las Vegas."

"Well, if this theatre is any indication of what you do on stage, I can only imagine what a show is like," I said. "Do you have clowns, too?"

She laughed. "Yes, all that and clowns, too," she said. "Look, I don't think I can explain it all to you in five minutes. And I have several meetings today. But I'll tell you what: Why don't you come to the first show tonight, at seven-thirty? If you'll give me your business card, I can have a ticket waiting for you at the box office. You can see what Cirque du Soleil is for yourself."

"That'd be great," I said, standing up and handing her a card. "I really appreciate it."

"Good. Then I'll see you tonight," she said. And with that, I gazed around the grand space one more time and took my leave.

. . . It's Easy to Find It.

I returned to the seminar with renewed energy, but not for "Creative Marketing." As another speaker started his presentation, my thoughts wandered back to what I had just seen. None of my colleagues seemed to suspect that while I might be sitting among them, an alert expression on my face, my mind had never truly left the KÀ theatre.

As we left the seminar, some of my colleagues began making calls for a quick nine holes of golf, while others discussed dinner plans. But I declined all offers.

"Doesn't sound like you, Frank," Steve said with a grin. "You feel all right?"

Reluctant to divulge my secret, I simply said, "I've got a ticket to see a show tonight."

"Which one?"

"The Cirque du Soleil show," I answered. "KÀ, I think it's called."

"Those shows are booked solid for months," Steve said. "How'd you swing that?!"

"I . . ." Hmm. How *did* I swing that? Why did Diane give me a ticket? Why didn't she simply kick me out of the theatre in the first place? When I saw the look on my colleagues' faces, it dawned on me how fortunate I was to have found those white doors and to have kept passing through them.

"Boys, if you know what you're looking for," I explained with false bravado, "it's pretty easy to find it."

chapter two

The Invitation

KÀ

The mysterious ambience of the darkened theatre, the crescendo of the music, the kaleidoscope of lights, the mesmerizing figures swirling on the stage had taken hold of my senses. I was no longer thinking about where I was and what I was witnessing. I was simply experiencing it.

Every journey inward begins with technique, but it can only progress if you allow yourself to move beyond the mechanics and into the moment. A skilled masseuse may begin by working on your muscles, but if you allow yourself to surrender to her touch, she will do nothing less than send you sailing off to some tranquil island. A hypnotist, I understand, simply by controlling the timbre of his voice, can lull you into your subconscious until you've forgotten all about your guide, so lost are you in the layers of your dreams. And a storyteller, by mastering metaphor, can weave a tale that will change your life.

The tale I was watching unfold onstage was an epic about a young prince and princess—twins separated in childhood without knowing whether the other was still alive. In one scene set on a sinking royal vessel, the young princess is swept overboard after narrowly surviving an attack that claims the lives of most of her family members.

As I watched her silent, solitary descent into the cerulean sea that the set had become, I wasn't thinking about how I'd gotten here—the convention seminar, the seven doors, the surprising generosity of Diane, who'd taken the empty seat next to me in the KÀ theatre just seconds before the show began. I was just watching, listening, feeling.

The translucent curtain draped in front of the stage and the spinning dive of the acrobat created the unmistakable sensation that I really was watching the princess plunge into a bottomless ocean. As she tumbled downward, my thoughts began their own descent as well, to Mike, my best friend who'd died the year before in a car accident.

Mike and I had swum together on our college team. I remember meeting him every morning at dawn, hours before practice began, just to get some extra laps in. When I think about the way I have to drag myself out of bed these days, I can't believe I'm the same person who used to welcome daybreak workouts. Mike had a lot to do with it; he was the only person I knew who wanted to win as much as I did; sometimes it's easier to let yourself down than to let down a teammate.

When I found out he had died, I thought about quitting my job. Mike was always saying life was too short to do something you didn't feel passionate about. But I couldn't bring myself to do it. What if I couldn't find anything else? What about the mortgage, the bills? And so, just a day after consoling Mike's tearful wife at his funeral, I was back at my desk.

I couldn't imagine KÀ had been scripted to stir up such memories, but oddly, that's what it felt like. Each scene seemed to provoke a different memory or feeling. Were the other members of the audience affected in the same way?

When the royal siblings were finally reunited at the end, the crowd answered my question by jumping to its feet to give the cast a standing ovation. I was swept along with the others.

As the lights came up, I glanced at the program Diane had given me. I noticed that there were no individual stars listed, no name touted above any other. Yet I'd just seen the artists perform feats of athleticism that most of my clients would never dare, even with a multimillion-dollar sports drink endorsement tied to it.

"Like it?" Diane asked, smiling. I turned to her, unable to speak. But I sensed that I didn't need to.

As we got up from our seats, I felt rejuvenated. I had been amazed at the way the artists had performed those risky, midair maneuvers with such incredible control. They weren't merely hitting their marks; they were using their bodies to sculpt stories, to carve ideas out of thin air, to evoke the audience's emotions. While watching the aerialists scale the nearly vertical revolving platform I'd discovered earlier that day, I had looked down at the small paunch that had developed around my waist over the last few years, the result of too many high-priced dinners wooing clients and late nights at the office fueled by fast food. I thought of how I'd landed my first major deals for our marketing company: by sharing stories about my own limited athletic experiences with prospective clients. Nowadays, our conversations seemed to revolve around one thing: money.

But despite my self-consciousness, I also felt a new sense of possibility: If these artists could contort their bodies into such impossible shapes, if they could leap from such astonishing heights, if they could make me feel a spark of something I hadn't felt in years, what was I capable of accomplishing in my own life?

"Would you like to come backstage?" Diane asked as we filed out of the theatre.

I hesitated; the show had cast such a spell on me, I was afraid I'd break it by sneaking behind the curtain and discovering that the Great and Powerful Oz was just some guy with an amplifier. But then I realized I'd gotten this far by ignoring my "better judgment" in favor of my instincts. "Sure," I said. "Let's go."

The Importance of Wrong Doors

We lost the throng shuffling out of the theatre by slipping through a door off to the side. After stepping into the same hallway I had discovered earlier that day and walking past a dry-erase board filled with what looked like notes for the performers, we climbed some stairs and turned into a living room set where the artists, still in their makeup and costumes, were hugging, hollering, and high-fiving.

It didn't occur to me, based on the seemingly flawless performance I witnessed that night, that they could be anything other than completely certain of their success, but seeing them rejoice reminded me that everyone has good nights and bad nights, that even the most seasoned artists have to take chances. And in this show, they were taking some pretty big chances: jumping from one pole to another thirty feet away, using only their thighs to save them from a six-story drop.

At different moments during the show, the performers would be swept beyond the audience's view, seemingly falling off the ends of the earth. Now that I'd regained the power of speech, my questions began bubbling to the surface. "Diane, where do they go when they drop off the stage?"

"They land on a huge airbag under the revolving platform," Diane said. "It's a sixty-foot drop. I wouldn't recommend it without a little training."

When the performers noticed Diane, they rushed over to her. She clearly had some influence here.

The artist who played the "Firefly Boy," the character who saved the princess from falling, gave Diane a big hug. "Slava!" she exclaimed. "Fabulous!"

She turned to me after Slava was pulled back into the crowd by one of his fellow performers, and said, "He's the fourth generation of a famous circus family in Moscow. For the Russians, performing is often a family tradition."

Another hug, this one from an Asian acrobat. "Henry!" She told me, "Henry was a regular nineteen-year-old kid from Edmonton when he enrolled in the National Circus School in Montreal. He had no real background in acrobatics, but he was determined to get here. You'd be surprised at how many stories there are like that. Most people who come to Cirque are pretty normal—they just have aspirations for something more."

I was surprised to see so many people backstage who were clearly not in the show—or not on the stage, at least.

Two of these men—their work clothes appearing almost exotic among the samurai-like archers in wild war paint and crimson and black costumes—walked up to Diane and gave her a hug. Diane introduced them to me: Ian, a brawny, bald man with a clipboard in his hand, and Rick, a lean, athletic guy in jeans and steel-toed boots, a bulky walkie-talkie on his belt.

"So, what happened?" Diane asked them. I had no idea what she was talking about.

Ian rolled his eyes. "Are you sure you want to know?"

"No, I probably don't," she said. "But whatever it was, you must have gotten it straightened out pretty fast. I don't think the audience had any idea something was off."

"Diane, I have to tell you, we were five minutes away from canceling the show. The stage lifts weren't working!"

"You're right—you shouldn't have told me!" She laughed. "Well, at least your checklist worked. Your protocol is a lot tighter now than it was during the fall previews."

"True," Ian said. "We would never have figured out the problem fast enough a few months ago."

"So, what was it?"

"A computer glitch," Steve said. "We were receiving a signal indicating that we had no hydraulic pressure in the lifts. When the lifts get that signal, right or wrong, they won't move. So the whole crew went down our checklist to determine what the problem could be, and we found it in a couple minutes. Well, actually, our automation whiz, Ian, found it." He patted Ian on the back. "A few months ago, we'd be trying to fix the entire hydraulics system, and not simply the computer that runs it." Rick turned to me. "The trick is, not trying to solve the problem before you've figured out what it is."

Ian added, "Do you know the definition of a good show?" I shrugged. "A good show is one where only *we* know what went wrong!"

"Well, I think you did a great job," Diane said. Then she turned to the entire group and called out, "Congratulations, everyone! Another one down, and only a few thousand more to go!" Their cheers still ringing in my ears, I followed Diane down the long white hallway, back out into the casino.

"Diane, I have to ask: Why did you invite me tonight? I mean, I'm just some guy who stumbled through the wrong door. You can't invite many strangers behind the scenes like this."

She pondered my question for a moment. "You're right, of course, I don't," she said. "I suppose I recognized something in you. And you know, I believe in the importance of wrong doors, of serendipity. I can't help but think you bumped into me for a reason.

"When we talked this afternoon," Diane continued, "you said that when you began your career, it felt like a calling, but now it just feels like a job. Not many people feel their job is a calling. Even fewer realize when they've lost that feeling. Tell me, what's different about your job and what you saw here tonight?"

"My job is nothing like what took place here tonight. I work behind a desk, even if it is with some of the world's most famous athletes. Most of the time, I'm negotiating contracts on the phone with huge corporations. I don't put on cool costumes and perform before a thousand people. I wear a suit!"

She laughed. "Our lawyers negotiate contracts, too, and our marketing people deal with the same corporations you do. But they probably don't do those things the way you do. Everyone here does things a little differently, no matter what their job. And they stay connected to our final product, the shows themselves. We don't run an assembly line, with people sealed away in their cubicles. Everyone is part of what we do on stage, which is why you see so many regular folks backstage tonight. I thought inviting you here tonight might help you remember your calling—what you were like before you put on that suit."

I looked reflexively down at my attire. Diane smiled; she had been speaking metaphorically, of course. Before I could reply, she said, "Frank, I have a lot of people to meet with tonight. But I'd like to stay in touch. Here's my card. If you're ever in Montreal, give me a call. I'd love to find out if you've been able to regain your passion. In a way, that's what Cirque du Soleil is all about."

I looked down at her card as she vanished from sight: *Diane McKee, President, Creative Content Division, Cirque du Soleil.*

chapter three

The Audition

Welcome to Cirque du Soleil

When I'd first returned to Chicago, I assumed the spell that Cirque had cast over me would fade just as predictably as my occasional resolution to get back into shape was quickly forgotten once my eyes fell upon a rich slab of chocolate cake on the dessert tray. And so I waited for the inspiration I felt in Las Vegas to evaporate, for my life to return to its quotidian pace.

A day passed, then another, and yet my excitement didn't fade. A week went by, then two—until I ultimately concluded that the fire Cirque had sparked in me would not be so easily extinguished.

It was with that in mind that I began sifting through my e-mail and the files on my desk one day, looking for a plausible justification for a trip to Montreal. And I found one: Cari Schultz, a collegiate gymnast we represented who had recently signed on for an audition with Cirque du Soleil.

Typically, such a client would be handled by one of my junior colleagues. Someone in my position usually represents only the big-money athletes—professional football, baseball, and basketball players—but I had lost all taste for the usual. For the first time in years, I began to appreciate the opportunities my job afforded me. I fished around my desk for Diane's card, picked up the phone, and started dialing before I could reconsider.

To my surprise, she picked up the phone herself. She remembered me immediately and asked when I was coming up to visit. "Next week," I blurted out, telling her about Cari Schultz's audition. When I hung up, I felt a huge weight lift from my shoulders—and I knew I'd made the right decision.

Although I had never met Cari before, by the time our plane took off from O'Hare Airport, the gymnast had already made quite an impression on me. Short, pretty, and strong, she reminded me a bit of Mary Lou Retton, the former U.S. Olympic champion. I soon learned she had as many questions about Cirque as I did.

"I mean, I'm not even the Big Ten champion, let alone an Olympic medalist," she confided to me as our plane climbed to its cruising altitude. "And Cirque hires world-class gymnasts. Why would they want someone like me?"

"They need talented performers," I explained, recalling my conversation with Diane the week before, "but I gather talent alone is not enough for them. They've turned down a few Olympic medalists over the years. It's more than just how well you can do the vault or the uneven bars."

"So what *do* they want?" she asked.

"I can't say for sure, but I know they like the fact that you do all the events—versatility is a big plus—and that you're the captain of the team. Because their performers have to work together for years, teamwork counts. I'm sure they got a sense of your personality from your phone interview."

"Oh gosh!" she said. "It was the strangest interview I've had all semester! They asked me to tell them my most embarrassing moment."

"What'd you tell them?" I asked out of curiosity.

She laughed. "The time my leotard split during my floor routine, right up the side almost to my armpit. It didn't show anything, but everyone in the arena was watching me when I finished!"

"What'd you do?"

"What *can* you do?" she asked. "I nailed my landing, threw my arms up in triumph, and gave them a big grin. The crowd loved it!" she said. "And the judges gave me the highest marks of my career! The Cirque scout loved it, too. She said that every accident is just a creative opportunity in disguise."

We were both laughing now. "I don't think it's hard to understand what they see in you," I said. "To be honest, I've only seen one Cirque show. But while the acrobatics are amazing, they're performers, not competitors, and passion and tenacity go a long way."

"I hope so," she said, gazing out the window at the snow-blanketed Canadian landscape below. "I've accepted the fact that I'm never going to the Olympics. But this is a wonderful opportunity to use my training in a completely different way."

Although it was early April, when we stepped outside the airport, we were met with a bracing twenty-degree chill, despite a radiant sun and cloudless sky. As our cab carried us to the Cirque headquarters in the city's north end, I saw snow piled up on the curbs, creating ramps big enough to launch a snowboarder. We soon pulled up to a sprawling campus adorned with a shiny aluminum cube in its center and a huge bronze sculpture of a clown's shoe in front of the main entrance.

After walking through the glass doors of the main building, I spotted Diane, wearing her signature suede jacket, at the security desk.

"Bonjour, Frank and Cari! Welcome to Cirque du Soleil!" she said, opening her arms wide. She gestured to the young woman standing next to her. "This is Marie, who'll be walking Cari through the registration process. You'll be staying across the street at the artists' residence," she told Cari. "And you," she said, pointing to me, "will be going on a little tour! But first, you'll both need to get your visitor ID cards."

Cari and I were led to a counter as bright and shiny as a beach concession stand to have our photos taken. "Please put your feet on the footprints," the photographer said, "just like at your Department of Motor Vehicles."

When I looked down to make sure my feet were on the right spots, I saw that the footprints were those of a clown, with tiny heels and huge feet. I couldn't help but smile.

After the camera clicked, I wished Cari luck, as I had done with so many clients before. When she smiled back, I realized that, this time, I meant it.

The Reason for Our Work

"We opened our headquarters in 1997," Diane explained while walking from the main foyer. "We'd been downtown in an old locomotive repair shop for years, and knew we needed more space. So we built this complex, thinking we would not outgrow it for at least a decade. But we ran out of space in just three years, so we doubled our space with another structure attached to this one, and we outgrew that in two years!"

We walked past a few circular, stainless-steel tables at which people sat sipping coffee, nibbling on croissants, and engaging in lively conversation. Everyone seemed to be talking animatedly, laughing, doodling on large sketch pads, scratching notes in their planners.

"Seems like a friendly place," I said.

"Oh, very friendly," she said. "Not all the time, of course—we have our moments, and people are people—but most of the time. The better we get along, the more free we are to let loose and express our ideas and emotions. It's hard to be creative in isolation. True creativity requires collaboration . . . and yes, even conflict and confrontation."

Diane led me through a sun-splashed hallway bordered

by a bank of large windows on one side and a series of colorful posters on the other, each with a quirky name: *Quidam, Saltimbanco, Varekai.* They sounded foreign, though I couldn't place the languages. The posters featured odd, arresting images: a headless man carrying an umbrella, a comical woman in full circus makeup smiling giddily, and a gangly, avuncular-looking man who appeared to be growing out of some sort of plant—until I realized that the plant was his pants.

Diane noticed my lingering gaze. "You'll see our show posters all over the building. It's important to remind people that whatever they do for Cirque du Soleil—whether they're acrobats or accountants—these shows are why you do what you do. It helps keep us motivated."

Never losing sight of the reason for your work—it was an idea I felt certain any business could benefit from. I tried to recall the last time I'd been to one of my players' games—or, more tellingly, had taken one of my assistants out to see a client play. I was dismayed to realize it had been years.

We hopped on an elevator, rode up a couple of floors, and walked down another hallway. A half-dozen framed photos lined the wall. My eyes were drawn to a glossy color picture of a man in a suit calmly reading a newspaper, a bemused smile on his face, while his clothes and hat blazed in flames.

"These are our clowns. The big baby you see there is in *Mystère*, our first resident show in Las Vegas. The crazy-looking kid is the clown from *Saltimbanco*, which is in Europe now. And the guy on fire is in "O," another Vegas show. That's real fire, by the way. He has ninety seconds to get across the stage without burning his skin—and I've never seen him panic and run!"

She took me past some of the meeting rooms, which were identified by show names as well: *La Nouba*, *Nouvelle Experience*, and *Zumanity*. A few rooms overlooked one of the big rehearsal studios, which must have been six stories tall. With no frosted glass or steel doors to block the flow of light or people, the atmosphere was open and inviting. As we walked past several offices, I overheard spirited discussions punctuated by occasional bursts of laughter.

"Let's go to . . . *Quidam*," Diane said. I sat down in one of the eight upholstered chairs and looked out of one of the windows. My head snapped back in disbelief when I thought I saw someone materialize briefly on the other side of the window before disappearing. When he rebounded back into the window frame a moment later, I realized I was not hallucinating.

Diane explained that the artists were rehearsing for the new show in the studio next door.

Standing up, I walked over to the window and pressed my face against the glass like a kid at a car wash. The entire Cirque du Soleil headquarters reminded me of a fantastical playground; it was like seeing the world through the eyes of a child. In the training studio below us, a few of the artists were strapped into some kind of harness, with elastic cords on each hip. They were bouncing thirty or forty feet in the air, flipping, turning, spinning, then grabbing on to trapezes attached to the ceiling—before releasing again, in unison, in pairs and trios.

"I hate to interrupt your reverie, Frank, but we do need to go over Cari's contract," Diane said, looking at some papers on the table. "If it's too much of a distraction, I can close the blinds."

"No! No," I said, reluctantly returning to my seat, unable to take my eyes off that window.

"I'll let you in on a secret," she said in a conspiratorial tone. "In tough negotiations, we hold our meetings in here, because once a phone company or computer manufacturer or accounting firm sees what we do, they want to be a part of it."

I could certainly understand wanting to be a part of it. What a fresh way to persuade a potential partner. Using this kind of creative approach when wooing clients at our agency would probably be more effective than the same tired speech about quality, reputation, and integrity.

"Not that Cari's contract will be tough." She smiled. "At this stage, the contract is pretty straightforward. If Cari passes the audition, she will spend twelve to sixteen weeks here in our general training program, where we will test her physical abilities, her versatility, her energy, and her openness. She will receive a flat weekly fee for her work. If it works out, we may offer her a position on one of our shows, and then we will talk contract again—long-term."

Amazingly, Diane's preview of the process put butterflies in my stomach; I felt as nervous for Cari as I had been as a young man trying out for my college swim team. The innate excitement of my job was coming back to me.

Our business completed, she said, "Why don't we go downstairs and take a closer look?"

Passion Is the Key to Everything We Do

As we walked down the stairs to the first floor, I noticed that almost everything—the hallways and offices, catwalks and staircases—was set at an angle, creating the kind of dimensional illusions of Willy Wonka's Chocolate Factory. The ceilings in the common areas were some forty feet high, with suspension wires and cables and steel tubes running overhead. Art—from paintings to reliefs to sculptures—decorated almost every flat surface. The overall effect was futuristic and spellbinding, the way the future ought to be. If one's surroundings can help stimulate creative thought—as some claim—the ambience of Cirque must send employees' creative energy into overdrive.

As we made our way to the first floor, everyone we passed seemed to know Diane. She stopped frequently for brief chats and updates, as she had with the folks backstage in Vegas. She instructed one man to send "the souvenir program concept" to her office. She congratulated a tall East German woman named Birgit on her new son. As we walked away, Diane explained, "Birgit's preparing to return to her show, where she performs on the Chinese poles. She started back in after her maternity leave by helping us with a little coaching, but I think she'll be back on the poles in another month." Next, Diane assured a stressed-out director of creation that, yes, they'd be able to start the show on time, and within the budget, if they persevered—a reminder to me that this was not a playland but a for-profit corporation, with many of the same financial and production concerns as any other.

"Budgets and deadlines?" I joked. "I didn't think any of the normal rules applied here—including gravity."

"Oh, we've got budgets and deadlines, all right," she said. "Without them, I don't think we'd be half as creative as we are. They force us to come up with solutions we'd never think of otherwise. Constraints on time, money, and resources can be incredible motivators! Some of our most inspired ideas have arisen from the most Spartan situations."

One thing was certain: Although the Cirque employees dressed casually, they were all working hard. When I mentioned this to Diane, she said, "Oh yes. I think you'll find this is a very hardworking crew—not just the artists, but everyone. One of our lawyers, Julia, puts in more hours at Cirque than she did at a major law firm, which was known for its grueling pace. She does it not because she has to, but because she loves it. She's passionate about what we do. I think most of us are. But it's not for everyone. Some people want more structure, more security, fewer demands on them personally to produce something special. And those people usually figure it out in the first few months. Passion is key to everything we do, and those without it don't last long."

A New Way of Thinking

We arrived at two gigantic red doors with round windows, and pushed through to enter an expansive practice gymnasium—a studio, as Diane referred to it.

My eyes were immediately drawn to the bungee ballet, with artists suspended from a grid overhead by elastic cords. Watching the six of them fall to within ten feet of the floor, then rocket upward toward the ceiling, where they seemed to become weightless, made my stomach sink in fear. But I could not look away. The speed, the energy, the precision and poise were extraordinary. The performers' coach, however, appeared less impressed than I was.

"Alex, this is not a solo act!" he yelled out to one of them. "We only have one month left—this will not do! You must pay attention to your partners. You must sense the rhythm, you must feel it and respond to it! Only then can you express yourself to the audience. It should appear effortless, so the audience can feel they are soaring with you! Now, let's try again."

The artists grabbed their trapezes again, while their coach gestured for the music to begin. After a few movements on the bars, they all jumped off their trapezes, backward, as if diving off ten-meter boards, reaching out for the water. But there was no water—only a cold, hard floor below—so when they hit the bottom of the bungee cord's reach, they flipped over and prepared to be launched skyward.

I noticed that six riggers—one for each performer— were constantly adjusting the tension on the safety lines, giving the artists enough slack to do their work, but enough security to ensure they'd be protected if anything went wrong. The six artists—two men and four women— could afford to be oblivious to the riggers' work. Instead, they focused on flowing through the air like synchronized swimmers. "Yes, yes, Alex, that's it!" their coach yelled. "Now, enjoy it! Give it to the audience!"

And they did—a sextet soaring through the air, falling and flipping, slipping past one another, acrobatic angels dancing on the clouds. The routine culminated with all six landing on their trapezes at the same moment, swinging gently as if doing nothing more difficult than dangling from a tire swing. The coach exclaimed: "*This* is what we've been working for! Now you can see what we have imagined! And now you can understand why people will want to see you again and again!"

We all clapped, and Diane called out, "Bravo!" which the coach took as his cue to approach us. Diane introduced him as Igor.

"Well done, *drug*," she said, using, as I would discover later, the Russian word for friend.

"*Spasiba*," he replied, bowing a bit. Igor, who was no more than five feet six, had a long salt-and-pepper beard and a broad smile to go with his intensely penetrating eyes. If he were dressed in vest, jeans, cowboy boots, and hat, he'd look like a character actor playing an ornery prospector in a B Western.

"They're looking great!" Diane said. "I see a lot of progress!"

"We're getting there," he said, sweat visible on his forehead. "But we'd *better* be making progress. The premiere is in a month—and we're only halfway there."

"It looks amazing," I said.

"*Nyet*," he said, waving off my compliment like an irritating fly. "We need to get it right every time. It needs to be tighter, so no one in the audience thinks about the hard work that goes into it. It should look natural. Look around us," Igor said. "This building is fantastic, such a magical place. It is like no other building I have ever seen. That took lots of imagination to build, of course, but without discipline—the discipline to learn physics and biomechanics, to insist on the best materials, to design and construct everything correctly—it would all fall down!

"Alex here is one of the most talented acrobats we've ever recruited," Igor continued, "but this is his first time working in an ensemble. And he's having a hard time realizing that what we do at Cirque is not mere athletics. We want *artists!* There is an important difference—one that took me a long time to understand.

"In a Cirque show, anything you can imagine, you can do. But this incredible freedom is both the problem and the solution. It requires you to think differently, and that can be difficult. As a former gymnastics coach, I had to learn to turn the acrobatic elements into artistic elements, to not simply settle for oohs and aahs but to elicit a more personal response from the audience."

I thought back to the powerful emotions that had washed over me at KÀ and realized it was no accident. It was part of their intent.

"So how do you help the athletes make the transition?"

"Have you ever done any coaching yourself?" Igor asked.

"A little," I said. "High school swimming, years ago. And even though I'd mastered the strokes, it took me a long time to learn how to convey what I had learned to my team."

"Exactly," Igor said. "Coaching at Cirque was hard for me at first—I had to learn a new way of thinking. I knew I was a good coach, but mainly because I'd learned from other good coaches. Cirque challenged me to apply my coaching skills to a completely different kind of performance. But the really challenging thing is to change the mentality of the performers I work with. Many of our performers are former competitive gymnasts. Gymnastics is essentially an individual sport. Gymnasts never have to think creatively or be a part of a true team. They got here by being strong *individuals*. So, right from the start, we really challenge ourselves to erase the lines between athletics and artistry, between individuals and the group. We need to transform an individual into a team player everyone else can count on, literally with their lives; and transform an athlete into an artist who can bring complete strangers to tears just through his body language.

"The other thing I had to learn," he said, "was that this is a business, an extremely complex and costly business. In Olympic sports, if you fall short, you recover and you come back. But this company is a private enterprise, with a tremendous amount of money invested in each show. Just one flop, on the scale at which we are working, would do tremendous damage to the company. Around here, you can earn enough credibility over the years to make one or two mistakes. But you also have to deliver. And you can't deliver without taking risks—individually or as a troupe. It is essential. But you have to learn to take the *right* risks— risks that will allow you to fulfill your vision."

Taking Risks

As Diane led me across the studio toward a group of nervous-looking athletes, I spied Cari standing toward the back. Seeing her, I remembered how tense, awkward, and embarrassing tryouts could be, especially among complete strangers vying for a spot on the team.

"Now, zis is what I want!" explained the acrobatic scout, with an exaggerated accent and a mischievous grin. The woman's name was Annie; Diane told me she was a former gymnast, choreographer, and national team coach. "You must climb zis rope here, zen, at ze top, you will sing a song! Are zere any questions?"

The two dozen candidates laughed nervously. Finally, a young man wearing a T-shirt from a gymnastics club in Italy asked, "You're serious?"

All humor drained from Annie's face. She put her hands on her hips and walked very slowly over to him. "Do I look serious?" she asked him. His eyes widened in surprise. "Do not be fooled by my sweet disposition," she told the group, getting another laugh. "I am not always so warm and fuzzy. So who will be first? How about . . ." she said as if she were scanning the group, then settled on the Italian man. "You, *monsieur, allez-up!*"

Everyone laughed. As the young man prepared to climb the rope, Annie asked, "What is your name?"

"Giovanni," he said. "But my friends call me Gio."

"Zen I will call you Giovanni," she said.

"I've competed for almost twenty years," he complained, "and I've never had to climb a rope before."

"Well," she said, throwing the rope toward his chest, "you do now, don't you?" Again the group laughed, although they clearly sympathized with the young man.

Gio protested, "But I can't sing!"

"Yes, Giovanni, and I cannot play ze flute! But if Cirque asked me to play it, I would!"

Giovanni got the hint and jumped on the rope. He struggled to get the hang of it, but after a few feet, his natural athleticism took over and he made his way twenty feet to the top quickly.

"Now, your song, please!"

"But all my songs are in Italian!"

"I don't care if they're in Sanskrit!" she said. "Sing!"

He cleared his throat and started belting out a hammy version of "That's Amore," to the delight of the group below. Although he sang it badly, he sang it loudly, with gusto. The others below him applauded as Gio made his way down the rope.

"Not bad, Gio," Annie said, making some marks next to his name on a clipboard. "Not good! But not bad."

"Why is she having them do this?" I whispered to Diane.

"Most of these people are athletes. As Igor explained, they are used to following the rules, doing as they are told. They have to learn to get out of their comfort zones, to try something different and express themselves. They need to learn to connect with people in new ways. For us, that is at the heart of what our shows are all about—connecting. We need to find out who can do it—and who can't."

To my surprise, Cari volunteered next. She hadn't struck me as someone who would be so bold. But there she was, climbing the rope—slipping at first, until she learned to coordinate the actions of her arms and legs. At the top, red-faced from the effort, she stretched one arm out for dramatic effect and blasted the theme song of *Annie*. "The sun'll come out . . . tomorrow!" Her voice warbled and was badly off key, but that only seemed to make her rendition funnier and sweeter. The rest of the group was clearly on her side, laughing and cheering her on. "Thank you!" she said when she finished to a chorus of clapping. Then she cautiously descended the rope. When she got to the bottom, she was blushing radiantly—and grinning from ear to ear. I found myself brimming with pride. A quick glance around the studio proved that her smile was indeed contagious.

"Well," I said modestly to Diane, "she's probably a better gymnast than she is a singer."

"Maybe so," she said, still gazing at Cari with an appreciative smile. "But I'll tell you what's more important: She is very gutsy. And if a person is courageous and generous enough, we can teach them the rest. To me, creativity is, first and foremost, all about courage—a willingness to take risks, to try new things, and to share the experience with others. And that girl's as lionhearted as they come."

At the end of my stay in Montreal, Diane bid me good-bye, encouraging me to let her know how things were going for me. "Keep in touch," she said as I got into a taxi to drive to the airport. "And be sure to give me a call if you'd like to visit us again."

chapter four

The Apprentice

A Leap of Faith

As I waited at the train station, absentmindedly flipping through the sports section of the *Chicago Tribune*, I felt myself begin to drift off into the kind of catnap so many commuters slip into on their way to work.

Suddenly, I was awakened by the memory of a poster I'd seen at the Cirque du Soleil headquarters. It was an image of a man, sitting in a chair, much like the one I had settled into; wearing a suit, similar to my own; calmly reading the newspaper, as I had been doing a moment before. The only difference was that while he was perusing the news, his body was alight in flames.

Now fully awake, I remembered the reason that poster, among others, had been hanging on the walls of Cirque headquarters: so that everyone at Cirque would keep in mind the reason they were there, the purpose of their work.

It occurred to me that in the last several weeks I had all but forgotten why Diane had invited me to the KÀ premiere in the first place. Somehow, I had made a connection with her. Sensing the cloud of ennui that had come to overshadow my life, she had offered me a lifeline—a chance to reexperience the passion and mystery all around me. And I realized, as I stepped onto the train and took my seat, that I was starting to fall back into the same rut I was in before—sleepwalking through life, eyes half open, with no real sense of direction. Why had I chosen my profession in the first place? More important: Why had I chosen to live this way?

Diane had hoped to remind me who I was *before* I put on this suit years ago. But it had been so long ago; was it even possible? I recalled one evening sitting with Mike at our favorite bar, talking about what we were going to do with ourselves after graduation. Mike was so sure of himself; he'd already gotten a job as a teacher in Brooklyn, where he'd grown up. He had talked about teaching since we were freshmen; I envied his ability to know what mattered most to him and pursue it with a single-minded sense of purpose.

I was less certain of what I wanted to do. There were so many things I was interested in, places I wanted to travel, people I wanted to be. But I had no idea how to make *any* of my dreams come true.

"Frank," Mike had said with uncharacteristic candor, "you have to find something you care about enough to build your life around it."

That evening, I decided to turn my passion for the discipline and beauty of sports into a career, helping young athletes establish themselves professionally. As an agent, I could help talented athletes achieve their dreams, while working in a field that energized me. And that's what I did.

But time passes and passion fades.

Could it also be rekindled?

The train had come to a stop at my station. As I stood up and folded the newspaper under my arm, my mind was ablaze with the excitement of a new idea. Though bold and risky, it was something I had to do. As Igor had made clear, nothing of significance could be accomplished without taking a leap of faith. But first you needed a vision.

When I arrived at my office, I called the secretary of our company's president and asked her to set up a meeting for me. "Alan's free this afternoon, Frank," she told me.

A couple hours later, I found myself sitting across from Alan's desk with sweaty palms, waiting for him to finish up a call.

After we exchanged pleasantries, I took a deep breath, frightened at what I was about to tell my boss. I liked and respected Alan, but I hadn't given him any indication of how unhappy I'd been feeling about my work. So much of our profession was about keeping up appearances—both our clients' and our own. But it came at a cost; rather than genuinely working to help our clients, we were frequently too afraid to upset them—and possibly lose them—to give them the honest advice they often needed to hear. To add to my fears, Alan was known throughout the office for his hot temper. Then I thought about how brave Cari had been on the rope at the Cirque studio—singing at the top of her lungs to her fellow gymnasts. If she could take such a risk, so could I.

"I'm unhappy with my work here, Alan. And I realize I've been unhappy for some time."

To my surprise, Alan remained perfectly calm. "Actually, Frank, I've sensed that. Why didn't you talk to me sooner?"

"I guess I only realized it recently." I thought back to all I'd seen in Las Vegas and Montreal and decided to lay my cards on the table. I told him what I'd experienced in my time with Cirque—and what I'd come to recognize was missing in my job and my life. Just when I thought I'd said all a person needed to say to get fired, Alan stopped me.

"Well, what do you want to do about it, Frank?"

So I told him my plan. I wanted to take a monthlong sabbatical; during that time, I would take Diane up on her offer to visit Cirque du Soleil again. I would learn more about their culture and how to apply some of their magic to my own life. I would also use my time there, I explained, to play a bigger role in guiding the career of our new client, Cari. She had passed her Cirque audition and was now embarking on a rigorous training program that would help the Cirque coaches assess how she would fit in with the company. "I'm not sure what I'll learn. But I may come up with some new ways to help the athletes we represent."

Having touched upon all the rational reasons for my request, I took a deep breath before I got to the heart of the matter. "Alan, I know if I don't try to rekindle what made me care about this job in the first place, I won't be able to keep doing this much longer."

Alan nodded reflectively. "Frank, you've been a star performer for us for, what, twelve years now? If this is what you need to do to get back to the top of your game, how can I say no?"

Next I called Diane to discuss my proposal and, I hoped, win her approval. "I think I can learn a lot from Cirque that can help me bring more clients to you. But to be honest, Diane, the effect that this kind of opportunity would have on my career is only part of it. In just a few days, you and the others at Cirque have changed my life. I can only imagine how much I've yet to learn about teamwork and risk, passion and the creative spirit. I guess what I'm asking, Diane—*begging*, really—is, will you be my guide into the whole Cirque experience? Not just for a few days but a few weeks—to help me observe how your people work and train, so that I can understand what it feels like to be a part of this family? You've already opened so many doors for me—I'm asking you to open a few more."

Diane was silent for a moment. During this seemingly interminable pause, my heart sank. What was I thinking? How could I have made such a request? *Well, you've already thrown the dice*, I thought; *let's see how they land.*

"All right," she finally said. "But let me be clear about

one thing: I can't be your guide. At Cirque du Soleil, as in life, you will have many guides. Each person who comes to Cirque, whether to experience a performance or to train and work, lives his or her own unique journey. There is no secret formula for creativity. What you will experience or take away, I cannot say. And this will be no picnic, no holiday—you will have to pay your dues. Talking to our performers and staff is not enough."

"What do you mean?"

"So far, you've only skimmed the surface of what we do here. You have yet to understand the hard work that goes into our training. If you come to Cirque, you need to be willing to experience total immersion. Rather than being a mere observer, you are going to participate. You will need to pass the same tests and endure the same challenges that all our performers go through before they become full-fledged members of Cirque du Soleil."

Minutes later, the arrangements had been made. I would be staying in the artists' residence for three weeks, undergoing all the steps of Cirque training, though in condensed form. As Diane made clear, never before had Cirque opened its doors to someone who was not a prospective artist. I realized she was taking an even bigger risk than I was and could find no adequate words to express my gratitude. It was the opportunity of a lifetime. But what made it even more rewarding was that I had gone out on a limb and taken a chance. And the people I shared my crazy idea with received it not with contempt but compassion. When you finally give voice to your dreams, you never know what's going to happen.

Cross-pollination

After a month of furious workouts to prepare for my training, I was back in Montreal for my first week of the circus life. Upon my arrival at the artists' residence on a Sunday evening, Diane's assistant, Ann, showed me to my room. She advised me to turn in early, as I had a full day ahead.

After unpacking, I found a fridge full of fresh fruit, a Cirque ID card, and an itinerary for my time here. I didn't recognize any of the names of the coaches, instructors, or directors on the list. But I was struck by the broad range of people I'd be meeting—from creative directors to clowns. As Diane had promised, there was also a daunting list of activities, including training on the same bungee-trapeze I had seen on my first visit. Despite my fluttering stomach, I willed myself to sleep.

I awoke the next morning to a brilliant sun shining in through the bay window of my room. My first meeting of the day was with one of the charter members of Cirque's coaching staff, Bernard Lavallard.

I met him in the cafeteria at nine A.M. If there is such a thing as an aging French Canadian hippie, I had found him. Bernard wore a beret, small round glasses like those made famous by John Lennon, and a long, salt-and-pepper goatee. He told me he had been a serious gymnast in the sixties. "I did rings and the horse. I was very intense. I had a—how do you say it?—a crew cut. If you saw a picture of me then, I don't think you'd recognize me today. Of course, I am an old man now," he added, chuckling.

If he was an old man, he certainly didn't look it. With his strong, lean frame, he looked like he might still be able to perform many of the same skills he had mastered forty years earlier.

"I left Olympic training in the late sixties to become a clown!" he said, laughing at himself. "My father was so mad! But this is what I wanted to do. It was the spirit of the time. And when I met the founders of Cirque—of course, it was years before the troupe officially came into being—they were the same way, open-minded and free-spirited. But they were also very hardworking, very disciplined—and they had a vision. They wanted to create something special, something big, something new. And their energy was contagious!"

Cirque needed a gymnastics coach, Bernard told me, to give their circus more intensity, more excitement, more precision. "We didn't want to give them a floor exercise. We wanted to blow people's minds!" he said. "And to do that, we had to do things no one else was attempting."

It helped that he and the other founders shared the same vision—even if they didn't always agree on how to achieve it. "Oh, we could argue about almost anything," he said, smiling. "What costumes to use, what athlete to hire, whether they should turn to the right or left, if we should use a spotlight or a floodlight. But that's the point: We talked about everything. Our first idea was almost never our last. Ideas evolved, and combined with others, until they became more original, more creative. And when we were done, you really couldn't say whose idea it was. It didn't matter!"

At first, Bernard said, the creators studied other circuses. Later, they asked the artists to do the same. Over time, everyone at Cirque was drawing upon as many outside influences as possible, from almost every field—painting, film, music, you name it. This sort of cross-pollination, Bernard explained, was one of the keys to Cirque's extraordinary freshness and vitality.

"I cannot tell you how the mind works," Bernard told me. "Even my own mind! After all these years, all these shows, I still don't know where ideas come from. Sometimes they pop into my head at the strangest times, from out of nowhere! And sometimes the connections make no sense—like the time I woke up at four in the morning with a new concept for a tumbling act, inspired by a Brazilian band I'd seen the night before."

I knew a great many artists were inspired by ideas and events totally unrelated to their chosen field. And I was struck by how isolated I had become in my own life, how much I had cut myself off from outside interests that might have broadened my thinking.

"So how do you turn these random ideas into an act?"

"Deadlines!" He laughed. "Of course, they always come too fast, but without them, your mind is not focused. With them, on the other hand, your panicked mind starts coming up with crazy ideas it never would have otherwise. If you have two days to design a transition from a trapeze act to a trampoline, you will think of something!"

"Most people hate deadlines," I said. "It hadn't occurred to me that limitations could be a good thing. What sorts of things hold you back?"

"Red tape!" he exclaimed, shaking a fist in mock rage. "It's a huge obstacle for us. We are getting so big so fast that we always seem to need a few more rules here, a bit more paperwork there. After all, we have three thousand people working here now. But we must be careful, too. Every new layer of management, every new rule or form gets in the way. They deaden the magic—cut off the electricity of inspiration. If there are too many restrictions, you stop thinking about what you *can* do and start thinking about what you *cannot* do.

"Picasso did not ask for approval from the legal department before he started painting *Guernica*," Bernard added.

Through the Eyes of the Audience

As I left Bernard, I thought of what he'd told me. The constant sharing of ideas. The way their first ideas were never their last. The importance of deadlines. And something that resonated particularly with me—the danger of red tape. We'd lost some key clients in the last year to a hotshot new agency that always seemed to have the jump on us. Were we too slow coming up with pitches? Could tighter deadlines help us come up with fresher ideas? Had we become too rigid, too wrapped in red tape to break out of the same old mold?

With my schedule as my guide, I headed down a set of stairs to the cubicle-office of one of Cirque's artistic directors, Charina. An olive-skinned Spaniard with long, straight, jet-black hair, she exclaimed, "Pardon the mess!" while moving piles of drawings, magazine photos, and blueprints to clear a spot on her table. "We are creating a new show. It is sometimes a chaotic process!"

Though in her late thirties or early forties, she exuded the energy of a teenager. As the artistic director of two shows, one of her biggest challenges was keeping her artists alive artistically, she explained. "One of the shows I worked on was a traveling production, performing in the same city six days a week for a couple months, before moving on to the next city. The other was a resident show—ten shows a week, two a night! With any show, the question I always come back to is: How do I keep the artists fresh, even after they've been doing the same show a thousand times?"

"So how *do* you manage it?" I asked. Clearly, what Cirque performers did was infinitely more taxing than my job, but I imagined that even here there was the danger of falling into a rut.

"For one thing, I have to work as hard as I expect them to," Charina said. "I cannot fool them. I know of one director who would come backstage after the show was over and say, 'Great job!' But the artists knew he hadn't been there that night, and had only snuck in the back of the theatre for the last five minutes of the show. This might seem like a small thing, but it was a big deal to the artists. As a result, he lost his credibility with them, so when he told them they needed to work harder and rededicate themselves, they would not listen. Trust me: In this business—in all businesses—your people will rarely work harder than the boss. That's why my first decision was to be at every show. If they had to be there, I did too."

I nodded; one of the reasons I'd stayed in my job so long after my interest had waned was Alan, our president. He clocked more hours than any of us, and still showed a passion for our business that I found hard to match. But while his enthusiasm had kept me going, I never asked how I might do the same for others.

"The second thing I do is give them notes after each show about little things I noticed—what worked, what didn't, what's coming along. That way, they know I'm paying attention and their work matters. And I've learned not to give only negative notes. If you do that, after a while, whenever you give them a note, they just groan! So it's important to be positive, too.

"But the best thing I've done," she said, "is to help them see their work through the eyes of the audience. Whenever someone is not in the show that night—because of injury or when they just need a night off—I give them a ticket to the show, so they can see what the audience sees every night. I was surprised to discover that most of them had never seen their own show from the house. Some of them had never seen the whole show at all, even backstage!

"Watching a show from the audience lets them see how beautiful it all is," she continued. "They sit next to a woman seeing the show for the first time and understand why she cries at the end of the show! They finally see what they've been working for—why they're sweating, training, and rehearsing so hard. Before that, they would only focus on their act, on their role. They never realized that it is the ensemble—the whole show, with all its parts—that is so evocative. After just one night in the audience, the artists themselves are transformed.

"The same thing is true here in Montreal," she said. "If the cooks and the managers and the receptionists don't go down to see a rehearsal once in a while, they forget what they are working for. They lose their connection with the final product. And that is certain death, I think, in a creative environment such as this. That's when it just becomes another job. Maybe you are an accountant—but you are an accountant at Cirque du Soleil. You and what you do are special!"

It wasn't hard to imagine how her insights could apply to virtually any business, I realized. If you don't understand the role you play, how can you be excited about what you're doing?

No Compromise

My next appointment was in the training studio, where I would soon be learning the art of the bungee-trapeze. But before they would let me attempt it, I had to pass a few basic physical tests.

I'd been in the studio before, of course, but this time I was here as a participant, not an observer. I felt a small tinge of nervousness, the way Cari must have felt during her audition.

After changing into my sweats, I went inside the exercise studio to take a look around. Above me, I saw a collection of huge, colorful plastic balls resting in a net hanging from the rafters; a rope dangled down to the floor.

Then I saw a man standing in front of me by a treadmill, holding a clipboard.

Ivan Mikhailov, I would later learn, held advanced degrees in nutrition and physiology, and looked every inch the part, with a scholarly face and Sigmund Freud–style beard. My training, he explained, would begin with a cardiovascular test. I was to run for eighteen minutes on the treadmill. It didn't sound too hard. I started to become a bit apprehensive, however, when Ivan strapped a heart monitor around my chest.

He started the treadmill at a leisurely pace, and I had little trouble striding along. My pulse hovered at fifty-eight beats per minute. "Very good," he told me, staring at the monitor. After three minutes, however, he increased the speed and the angle of the treadmill; by the time I hit the nine-minute mark, my legs and lungs were beginning to feel the heat.

Over the next six minutes, Ivan cranked up the speed and angle repeatedly, pushing me right to my limit. My pulse was racing at 166, and my heart felt like it was on fire. No matter how fast I breathed, I could not get enough air. I was just barely keeping pace with the treadmill, hanging on by a thread. Sensing my exhaustion, Ivan put his left hand near my lower back to make sure I didn't rocket off the treadmill into the training tables behind me.

"Just ninety seconds more, Frank," Ivan said, giving me a rare note of encouragement. If the disarmingly candid conversations about instilling a culture of creativity that morning had a way of opening me up to new ideas, the intensity of the treadmill had a way of peeling back the layers of my personality. I no longer cared what I looked like, or what Ivan or anyone else thought. I was just dying to get through this, to get to the end. I had nothing left; but I was so close, there was no way I could quit.

"Three . . . two . . . one . . . You are done! Grab the handles, while the treadmill slows to a stop." I may not have set any records, but I had passed the first test.

The same could not be said for the exercises that followed. On the chin-up bar, adhering to the strict form all Cirque artists must use, I recorded half a chin up—just enough to get my feet off the ground. I was even worse on the rope test. I took hold of the rope, furiously throwing one hand over the other, again and again, until I looked up and noticed the ceiling had gotten no closer.

"Okay," Ivan said, "so the rope is not your thing." As if on cue, Olga, a dark-haired eighteen-year-old Russian acrobat, leaped on the rope and, using only her hands with her legs extended in a perfect V parallel to the floor, glided up the rope and then descended very slowly, using only one hand at a time. I was humbled, as if I were the kid picked last for a game of kickball.

"I'd had a few more things planned, but I think you've done enough for the day," Ivan said.

I picked up my belongings, along with the remaining shreds of my dignity, and headed for the showers.

"Ah-ah," Ivan shook his head. "No time for that. Diane tells me you've got an appointment with René. On the grid."

I wasn't sure I liked the sound of that.

I took the elevator to the sixth floor, where René was waiting for me. He wore a ponytail, a black T-shirt, black jeans, and black, steel-toed work boots.

"Frank, are you ready?!"

Still breathless from my shameful attempt on the rope, I could only nod.

René waved *This way!*, and I followed him through the short hallway onto a grid of high-tension wires, spaced about four inches apart, that sank a little when I stepped gingerly on them. Below us was six floors of air, and a very large, hard floor sprinkled with what looked like toy-sized people and props.

"I hope you are not afraid of heights!"

I smiled back. "No," I said, and it was true. I was not generally afraid of heights. "But I *am* afraid of dying prematurely and unpleasantly."

"Oh, but you have nothing to worry about!" He made a few small jumps on the grid, causing me to bounce a bit. "You see, we are perfectly safe. You must trust me."

I can't say I felt reassured. Soon enough, though, we fell into the comfortable routine of René talking and me listening. "Most of us riggers learned construction or welding or something else before getting into this line of work," he explained. "It takes a while for a new employee to learn how the circus works, and to learn how Cirque works. We expect the people we hire to have certain skills, but what they have to develop is a certain way of thinking. If you are just a great welder, you will not last here. It is not just construction skills we want; it's the artistic sensibility that allows you to create equipment that's perfectly integrated into the show."

"You mean, a balance between safety and the artistic?"

"No!" he said. "No! That is the most common misconception of what we do. There can be NO compromise on safety, and NO compromise on appearance. We must be a hundred percent safe, all the time, AND a hundred percent aesthetic. And that is what makes it so challenging. That's what forces us to be creative: no compromise!

"Look," he said, waving an arm over all the activity sixty feet below. "If they told us 'You just have to be artistic,' that would be easy! We'd let our artists fly all over the stage without safety lines, and shoot them out of canons, and it would be great fun—until someone got hurt . . . or worse. And if they said 'Just be safe,' that is easy, too! We would strap everyone into straitjackets, make them wear helmets, and never let them leave the ground. But it wouldn't be much fun to watch! So this is the hard part: The artists here must be able to perform the most incredible tricks in the world, yet never be in danger. *That's* what forces us to be creative, to find new ways to do both.

"And it's this trap, this contradiction, that inspires me," said René. "For example, in the show 'O,' the water show out in Las Vegas: We have 1.5 million gallons of water in a tank that is constantly moving and changing shape. Above the water we had to build an apparatus for the artists to swing and fly from—almost like a jungle gym of parallel bars and trapezes—only sixty feet in the air! But we couldn't just create some big, clumsy metal contraption. The audience would hate it! So we went to work.

"Our whole mind-set was: Everything must be integrated into the show, and *nothing* is impossible. It needed to be very light—we used fifteen different metals to build it!—and it needed to be very strong, easily holding a dozen artists exerting all their force on it. And it needed to be integrated into the show's theme of water. It also needed to be beautiful without upstaging the performers. We tried a lot of different ideas until we came up with the one that worked. We made the entire apparatus look and feel like a boat in the sky—one that even rocks back and forth when the artists swing on it. You have to get the mechanics of it right, then get the aesthetics right so it is not just a machine, but an environment that supports and feeds the artists' performance."

"I didn't realize," I finally said, "how much work went into the designs."

"Good!" he said. "We do not want to be the stars of the show; we want you to *enjoy* it. If you don't realize there is a three-million-dollar apparatus that took us two years to perfect hanging over your head, then we have done our job!

"You see, it is like this," he added, kneeling down on the wire grid and grabbing two of the wires we were standing on. "You have to be safe on the one side," he said, pulling one of the wires in to make the square a little smaller, "and artistic on the other," he said, pulling the parallel wire closer. "AND the equipment has to be integrated into the act," he said, pulling the third side in, "AND you have to make it so no one notices too much," he said, pulling the fourth and final side in. "This gives you a much smaller target, so you have to find new ways to satisfy all four."

As a result of René's manipulation of the rigging, I was now surrounded by wide gaps on each side of the little square he had created—just a foot or two from where I was standing.

"I . . . I didn't know these wires could move so much," I said, clutching the vertical I-beam with my right hand.

"Oh, yes, Frank, look at this!" He then proceeded to expand his little box into a four-square-foot hole in the wire grid, more than big enough for me to fall through to my death. "Actually, this can expand to six-foot sides, so we can raise big things from the floor onto the grid, and lower others back down. This is another good example of creating something new. This wire 'floor' is strong enough to hold twenty tons of stuff, yet barely weighs anything. And it's amazingly flexible!"—which he proved by bouncing on the wires. I clutched the I-beam with both hands.

"Aha, Frank, trust me, you are safe. This floor can hold you, no problem. If we can park a car up here, we can park you!

"Perhaps it is time to show you the shop." He began walking back across the grid to the elevator, then continued. "We have great freedom to think of almost anything, but we have great responsibility, too. Safety is not something they need to tell us to worry about, because we know, with eleven shows around the world, there are people entrusting their lives to our work twenty-four hours a day, seven days a week. That is not a responsibility to be taken lightly. We cannot let anything happen to them. Ever."

"With seven hundred artists in the air almost every day," I asked, walking behind him on the springy grid, "there must be incidents, occasionally, aren't there?"

"Incidents, yes," he said. "Occasionally. But very rarely. They do get injured sometimes, because they are athletes performing difficult acrobatic movements every day. However, it cannot be because of our work. If there is an accident—and we've had a few, but only a few—we fly out and conduct a thorough investigation. So far, it has usually been attributable to human error, like an unlocked harness or performance error; only very rarely is it related to equipment failure."

"So it's not your fault," I said.

"No!" René exclaimed. "It is *still* our fault, because it means we did not design it simply enough, or we did not train the artist well enough, or we did not stress to them enough how important double-checking their safety harness is. We cannot *afford* to blame the artist. It is too easy, and it would make us sloppy, knowing we can blame someone else. If something goes wrong, that means maybe we didn't provide the right system for them to use.

"Because our creations must be integrated with the work of the directors, the artists, and the lighting people, we are responsible for the shows, too. We are in a life-and-death business. We cannot simply say it is some other department's responsibility. When we design our equipment, we must remember that even world-class acrobats aren't technicians. We must make it simple, and easy, and consistent to use. You have to know your people, and the psychology that goes into the process."

"How can you make sure it's all going right?"

"We always have riggers on every show, all the time, watching everything, testing everything, double-checking everything. If we're responsible, we have to be there. I still go up on the sky-boat in 'O,' I still go on the Russian swing in *Saltimbanco*, I still go on the moving stage at KÀ. We have to find creative ways to test our systems, to make sure we miss nothing. But one of the most important things we have is our senses—our eyes, our ears, our instincts.

"You have seen KÀ, yes?" he asked.

"Yeah, it is the only show I've seen live," I said. "It made quite an impression!"

"Good! It should. You saw the tent on top of the cliff that turned into a mechanical bird?"

"How could I forget?" I said. "It was one of the most inspiring scenes of the night."

René smiled. He was not a man of great ego, but he clearly took pride in his work. "Well, when I was there a few months ago, we were flying the bird in rehearsal, sixty feet above the stage, with the music playing, and I heard a little click. The other people said, 'What are you talking about? I didn't hear anything.' But I trusted my gut on this. I stopped everything—the rehearsal, the music, the director—and had the bird brought down to the stage. The way it's built, it's steel on steel, nylon on nylon. Everything has a good vibration when it's running well. But this didn't sound right. Usually, something that's a little out of whack—that is on the verge of breaking—will give off a different sound, a different vibration.

"After we brought the bird down, I sent another rigger

up to the ceiling to check the shiv—the right pulley—and sure enough, it was falling apart.

"Diagnosing that was not engineering. That was instinct. If you just inspected everything by the book, you'd miss a lot. We riggers are not creative the way the directors and designers are, but if we don't bring some imagination to our work, if we behaved like robots, we would be putting our artists in danger. And we are allowed to use our imagination here! When I first designed that bird, no one told me my vision was faulty. No one said my ideas were crazy. I was given the freedom to build what I thought would work. And when it was time to fix it that day, no one said I didn't have the authority."

The responsibility that rested on René's shoulders seemed overwhelming to me. If I messed up at my job, maybe a few lawyers got a little aggravated, but no one got hurt, no one got killed. I could see how important it can be to trust your gut at times, no matter what you do. As René pointed out, we're not robots. When we fall into a routine, we're no longer bringing all our senses, our intuition, our complete attention to what we do. And these are precisely the qualities we must draw upon, particularly when they've been strengthened by years of experience.

A few months before, I'd tried to convince one of my clients, a young basketball star, to play in a high-paying, celebrity-studded, made-for-TV exhibition game instead of volunteering at a summer camp for underprivileged kids where he had gone himself. "Think of all the good you could do with the money you make from a week of work," I told him. "You could start ten camps of your own with what they'll be paying you." Yet I knew deep down, even as I spoke the words, that I was trying to convince myself as much as I was my client, all based on the promise of a hefty commission. And yet, I pushed away the small voice inside me that knew what I was doing was wrong. In the end, I wasn't fooling either of us, and I'll never forget what he told me: "Of course you'd see it like that. It's a good thing I don't." He walked out of my office and, the next day, left the agency and signed with our biggest rival. I had abused his trust and he knew it. In René's job, such failures couldn't be tolerated.

"With so much responsibility," I asked, "how do you sleep at night?"

"As long as I've done my job the right way, and my people have, too, I sleep very well," he said. "To relax, I go hang gliding."

"Hang gliding?!" I was incredulous. "That hardly sounds relaxing!"

"Well, think about it," he says. "If I'm playing cards, I'm going to start thinking about every nut and bolt we put together that day at work. But when I jump off a cliff at ten thousand feet, I cannot think about anything else now, can I? The world below melts away."

The Fear of Success

After saying good-bye to René, I walked to the locker room, my mind stirring with the ideas I'd learned throughout the day. I was grateful that my next appointment involved physical activity—anything to steer my mind away from some of the things I'd done at work that were no longer sitting well with me. René was right: Physical activities, even risky ones, worked wonders on the mind as well as the body. In college I used to go swimming whenever something was troubling me. But after I graduated, I made only a few halfhearted attempts to get back to the pool. Without the thrill of competition, it just wasn't the same. The month I'd spent preparing for my time at Cirque had reminded me how energized I felt after a good workout.

When I reached the locker room, I noticed a hanger with my name on it. Then I saw what was hanging from it: a lycra body suit with a harlequin pattern across the torso. How was I going to fit my middle-aged body into that?

After a few moments of tugging and stretching, I managed to get it on. I walked self-consciously into the studio to meet my bungee-trapeze instructor, the vivacious Tatiana.

Her black spandex tights and blue-and-white tie-dyed tank top showed just enough of her abs to let me know I was way out of my league.

"Hallo, Frank!" she said, radiating a hundred-watt smile. She launched right in. "Fifty percent of the people who try this can't reach the bar," she said, pointing to a white trapeze hanging from the grid ceiling similar to the one I'd just walked across with René. "And only twenty percent of those can make it over the bar and sit on it. Let's get you up over that bar! What do you say?"

"Ahh, sure," I said, exuding all the confidence of a fourteen-year-old boy asking a girl out on a first date.

"Let's get to work! Come on, Frank!"

I followed Tatiana to a nearby training room, where a bigger metal trapeze was suspended only eight feet or so above the floor.

"Now, grab the bar."

I was dubious. I'm five-eight, with a vertical leap that would barely clear a matchbox on a good day. But Tatiana was standing in front of me, hands on hips, staring at me expectantly. Who would want to fall short? I crouched down and jumped as high as I could—and just barely snagged the bar. A small victory.

"Very good," she said. "Now, once you have gripped the trapeze, you must swing back and forth with your legs, then plant your strongest foot on the bar. When you've got your foot on the bar, you're all set. From there, you only need to slide both legs through and over the bar, grip the bar behind your knees, grab the ropes, and pull yourself up." With a little help from Tatiana, I managed to climb on the trapeze and sit on it, gazing down on the floor a few feet below me.

"Okay, that is enough," she said. "I want to save your arm strength for the real thing." Perhaps she had talked with Ivan about my lackluster performance on the rope.

As we walked back to the main studio, I looked up to the ceiling and realized the trapeze suddenly looked a lot higher, a lot smaller, than it had just a few minutes before. René was waiting for me, to strap me into the safety harness. He tightened the belt a notch or two more than I would have liked, squeezing any extra pounds I still carried over the belt. But by now, after the conditioning sessions, I had given up any illusion of vanity. Self-consciousness, I concluded, is something you have to let go of if you expect to take flight.

Next, using carabiners, they attached four or five huge elastic bands—bungees, basically—to each side of the harness and began hoisting me up by another rope attached to a pulley. "*Bon voyage*, François!" René said. As I rose up to twenty-five feet—which might not seem like much until you find yourself suspended from such a height with nothing between you and the floor—I noticed that the artists rehearsing below had all stopped to watch me. But the higher I rose, the smaller they became, and before I could register my embarrassment, they were too far away to worry about.

"Now, Frank," Tatiana urged me, "you must begin to bounce to reach the trapeze! Pull on the bungees while you bring your knees up to your chest. Yes, that's it!" I started bouncing up and down three feet, then five, then ten—until eventually, the feeling of weightlessness increased, and with it, the disorienting sensation that I was connected to nothing at all, just floating and flying in the air. My hands were clutching the bungees hard enough for my knuckles to turn white. When I increased my bouncing "span" to fifteen feet, then twenty, I realized I was dropping perilously close to the floor below—and flying amazingly close to the trapeze above.

I had never fully appreciated what "fear of success" meant until this moment. The closer I got to the trapeze, the more likely Tatiana was going to make me let go of the bungee cords and reach out for the bar—a thought that made my stomach churn.

"Just three more good bounces, Frank, and you'll have it!"

I didn't dare look up, or down, content to stare straight ahead. I was now unsure how far away the trapeze was, and I was afraid to find out.

"Now, Frank, now! Reach for the bar!" Ignoring every natural survival instinct in my body, I let go of those bungee cords, leaving myself entirely at the mercy of the harness René and Tatiana had fashioned for me, and reached out for the bar, which didn't come into view until the split second I was to grab it.

If you ever want to feel your heart leap up your throat, try lunging for a trapeze forty feet in the air that's just out of reach—so that you come careening back down toward earth a split second later, just long enough for you to wonder whether your harness is as secure as you hoped. After falling thirty feet, I finally felt the tension of the bungee cords kick in, pulling me back up to twenty-five feet, where I bobbed gently, safely.

"Very close, Frank! You can get it this time!"

I started the process again, bouncing up and down, pulling on the bungees as I brought my knees up to my chest. My rhythm improved, as did the corresponding height I achieved with each pull.

"Three more big pulls, Frank!" Tatiana called out, with everyone watching below. "One! Two! Three! Reach out!"

Once again, however, I fell just short; clearly, I was afraid of overshooting the trapeze—or perhaps just afraid of grabbing it. It's amazing how much we fear the unknown—even when the unknown carries with it the possibility of success. We are so determined to stick to our comfort zones that we learn to live with disappointment, as long as it's familiar and safe. This was the lesson, I knew, this training session was all about. Our fears hold us back, make us fall short of our goals. Only by taking risks can we hope to accomplish the extraordinary.

I watched my outstretched hands fly by the white bar, just a few inches shy of the mark—until I was once again plummeting to earth.

"Ohhhhhhh!" Tatiana said, leading a chorus on the floor. "Closer that time! Let's try some other things to rest your arms." Yes, I thought, she definitely had talked with Ivan about my rope test.

Tatiana guided me to a stationary position twenty-five feet in the air, then showed me how to do a somersault. "You must lean forward, Frank, with your head and shoulders, and then put your arms out, like Superman, and kick your legs up behind you." This sounded easy enough, until I realized it meant I would once again need to put complete trust in the harness's ability to defy gravity. Working tentatively, I couldn't generate enough momentum to make my body tumble forward. But remembering that I was oh-for-two on the trapeze, and that everyone was cheering me on, I took a bold leap into the unknown.

Magically, my head dipped toward the floor, my legs came around, and my body swung itself around on its own. It worked! Before I could think about what I was doing, I had done it!

"Yeah, Frank!" Tatiana did not have to tell me to do it again—I was dying to and I did, three more times. "Now do a double!" Before the words were out of her mouth, I was flipping my body forward with abandon, throwing myself headlong with enough speed to make two full rotations.

"Now the other way!" Tatiana bellowed. This was tougher. It required me to let go of the bungee cords again, which I was now comfortable doing, but also to tuck my knees in and toss my head *backward*, going into the somersault completely blind. I hesitated for a moment, but then fell back into the spirit of adventure I had relied on to flip forward—and voilà! I had done it again. And again, followed by a wicked double backward flip. I hadn't mastered the art of the bungee somersault, of course—but I had learned the art of trusting my coach, my rigger, and myself.

"Okay, Frank, ready to reach for the trapeze again?" I started bouncing up and down, getting ready to grab the trapeze, before I could compose an answer. Tatiana was smart; she had obviously known the somersaults would increase my confidence. I was going to go for it this time, I would hold nothing back. A little madness goes a long way, and I was wild with it. *I will not fear the height*, I told myself, *I will not fear the trapeze, I will just throw myself into the bouncing without any second thoughts.*

"Three more good bounces, Frank! That's one!" I was not going to back off this time. I was going to crank the best bounces I had ever done.

"Yes! Two!" I pulled with all my might.

"Three! Reach, Frank. Reach!"

At the apex of my bounce, almost forty feet from the floor, I finally looked up—and there it was, just a couple feet from my eyes! I reached, and grabbed the bar with one hand—against all of Tatiana's instructions. But I got it! I grabbed the bar with my other hand and soon was hanging from the bar! Before Tatiana could even remind me how to finish the job, I worked my body up so I was sitting on the bar. I was swinging back and forth like a schoolkid, waving to my friends forty feet below, cheering for me.

And then it was time for the scariest maneuver of all: falling off the trapeze *backward*, to avoid tangling the bungees in the trapeze. Well, I'd come this far, and things had worked out amazingly well. I rocked back and forth, and counted to myself: one, two, three—go!

I fell backward off the white bar, my head arcing its way to the floor, falling ten, twenty, thirty feet, as I watched the floor come closer, until—*boing!*—the harness and bungees saved me again. Before I knew it, I was bouncing comfortably in my old position, smiling at those below. I can't convey just how triumphant I felt at that moment.

When I stepped out of the harness, I realized I was sweating almost as much as I had been on the treadmill. My mouth was so dry, my tongue felt like I'd just licked Las Vegas sand.

"Well, how was it?" Tatiana asked.

"Great!" I said, exhilarated by my success in overcoming my fears and conquering the trapeze. It was not unlike the feeling I'd had when I'd summoned the courage to talk to Alan and Diane about coming to Cirque. "When can I go up again?"

That evening, Diane came by my room to see how I was holding up.

"How do you feel?"

"Tired," I admitted, "but excited, too. What a day!"

"Your eyes have a look of elation in them I haven't seen before. It's the look I'd hoped I'd someday see when we first met at KÀ. That is the power of the circus, of the imagination. It's what Cirque is all about, both for the audience and those of us who work here. We transform the dull and ordinary into something special and memorable, something that touches people's lives. And I believe we all have that power, no matter what we do. But only when you draw on some of what you've learned here today— about risk, collaboration, trust.

"You have to be willing to step outside your comfort zone and stretch beyond what you think you're capable of. At Cirque, we do that through our bodies and our performances. That was one of the reasons I allowed you inside Cirque du Soleil. As a former athlete yourself, I knew you would fit in. Of course, you don't have to be an athlete or an artist to reinvent your life, your work, or your world."

Diane congratulated me on a successful first day. "Now get some rest—you'll need it for tomorrow."

chapter five

Beneath the Surface

We Want You to Make Mistakes

When I awoke the next morning, it took me a few moments to remember where I was, but my aching muscles and joints soon reminded me. I had just gotten dressed after a long, hot shower when I heard a knock on my door. I opened it to find Cari standing before me, smiling enthusiastically. She told me she planned to use her day off to watch me go through the Cirque du Soleil gauntlet. I was flattered and embarrassed, because it occurred to me that, in recent years, I hadn't been as supportive of my clients.

"Are you ready?" she asked me.

I shrugged. "We're gonna find out."

Diane had arranged for me to work with Cirque du Soleil's head makeup designer. At first I balked at the notion of sitting through a three-hour makeup session. I wasn't going to join a show—so what was the point? Diane explained that, at Cirque, makeup is part of each artist's warm-up, gradually preparing them for the transition from daily life to life on stage. In other words, it was another way to express a more fundamental creativity—makeup isn't about concealing our faces and flaws, but about revealing another side of ourselves to the outside world.

Cari and I walked to the main building for my makeup session with Mademoiselle Claudia, a charming woman with short brown hair who looked to be in her late thirties. I took my seat between a huge Ukrainian athlete and a tiny Chinese girl.

"We've looked through our books of Cirque characters, and we've come up with one we think will fit you," Claudia said. She pulled a three-ring binder off a shelf, opened it to a page from *Quidam*, a traveling Cirque show, and pointed to the German wheel character. "His face was closest to yours in terms of bone structure, and I liked his energy. Outgoing, a little crazy—from what I hear, like you. What do you think?"

The character wore a turquoise-colored bowler that rested upon a shock of crazy blond hair; he had a white face with electric-blue eyebrows and red cheekbones. It was a bold look but had obviously been crafted with meticulous precision. I liked it.

"Let's do it," I said. Claudia laid the book out on the countertop and flipped through the pages, which contained step-by-step, illustrated instructions indicating how the character was to be made up.

"We put these books together a few years ago to ensure that each character would stay consistent from year to year, even if we change artists," she said. "But, of course, there is great room for individuality in each role. You never put makeup on exactly the same way twice."

I had never applied makeup before in my life. Even as a child dressing up at Halloween, I never wore the kind of ghoulish or exotic faces my friends picked, opting instead for some kind of jersey and a helmet. It was easy, safe, and the only makeup it required was a little coal underneath my eyes—poor preparation for today's task.

Claudia started collecting the various colors, brushes, and sponges we'd be using to create my new face. The goal for the artists was to learn how to apply the makeup themselves, as they would on tour, far from Claudia's guidance.

"As you can see, we will start by putting on the foundation, a base of white over your forehead, your eyebrows, your nose, around your mouth, and circling your chin," she said, dabbing a wedge-shaped sponge into a small plastic dish of pure white. "Here, now you try it."

I dabbed some makeup on my cheekbones, and I found it was surprisingly difficult to get the right amount on the sponge in order to spread it smoothly. "Do not press too hard, Frank, or drag it—you will stretch your skin. And if you do this every day, you will look too old too soon!"

While I started to apply the white base more artfully, Claudia told me about herself. "When I told my mom this is what I wanted to do, she just laughed!" Claudia said. "I had fallen in love with so many things—ballet, dance, skating, sculpture—she did not believe me anymore. But this time it was for real. I took courses in theatre, learning how makeup works together with every aspect of the theatre—the costumes, the lighting, the staging.

"I tried on a lot of different faces before I found the right one. And now I'm helping others find theirs. To me, that's exactly what the perfect job should be, a melding of our talents and our passions. That's what gives me—and all of us here—the energy to try to make something fresh, something new, all the time."

Claudia motioned for me to pause. "Okay—first we will add a light dusting of white powder on your face. The foundation is crucial to your character. Yet it is also the one element the artists are apt to neglect. When they skimp on the foundation, though, the strong lights on the stage wash out their makeup—the light cuts right through to their skin and the colors get lost."

"How long does it take the artists to learn how to do this themselves?" Cari asked, flipping through another of Claudia's books, absorbed in the possibilities the books represented.

"Well, the first time is very difficult. It can take three or four hours. Few of you artists can sit still that long!" Claudia said, "You are, after all, made to move. Some are so afraid of the first makeup session that they cannot sleep the night before. And these are people who do triple somersaults on the trapeze in front of two thousand people!"

At that moment, I could sympathize with them. I watched Claudia paint a crisp streak of Peacock LU-19 on my right eyebrow, then fade the top half to nothing in just an inch. Watching her carve a sharp, sweeping swath on my eyebrow, I realized I would never be that accurate. I tried in vain to re-create the same effect on my left eyebrow, but all I painted was an ugly, ill-defined blue smear. I took a deep breath and lowered my brush, discouraged. But Claudia had been doing this for years, I thought. I was not likely to nail it on the first day. So I picked up my brush once again.

When I finished, we both stared at the mess I'd made of myself in the mirror. "Um," I finally said. "This side doesn't look so good."

"Don't worry. It's important for our artists to make their mistakes here, while we're around, because they are sure to make them on tour when we are not there. With makeup, there are no mistakes—just different ways of getting to the final look."

I knew Claudia was right, of course. The greatest challenges I'd faced in my career occurred when Alan was not there to hold my hand. All he could do was teach me what he knew and trust me to use that knowledge myself.

Claudia signaled for me to stop. "When you draw these lines," she said, "you must *not* follow the lines on your face—they're false signs about how your face moves. Here, let me show you." Claudia picked up a plastic dish of Brick Red DR-5, dabbed it with a thick brush as any painter would, and told me to make a smile, then a frown. Next she drew an exaggerated outline of my "clown mouth" that didn't follow the lines of my face, and filled it in. "Now, smile," she said. I did—and the red lines fit perfectly, amplifying my smile so you could see it 200 feet away. "Now, frown," she said—and I was shocked to see a frown as deep and melancholy as my smile had been exuberant.

"That's amazing!" I said.

"You just have to ignore the obvious lines on your face and focus on your bones and your muscles *beneath* the skin. That's where your expressions come from, not your skin. Now, you try it."

Unlike my first clumsy attempts at the eyebrow, this time, it worked.

"Yes, now you're getting it!" she said. "You're not trying to paint *over* your face, you're trying to *bring out* the essential elements of who you are."

We moved to the cheekbones next, with Claudia feeling my face for the apex of my right cheekbone and the place where the three main facial muscles meet to form a small indentation in the middle of a triangle. She cut a sharp red line over the stark white foundation, from my ear to a point right below the center of my cheekbone. "The cheekbone is not straight; it is curved," she told me. "If you paint on the cheekbone, you will kill it." The horizontal line complete, she faded in the area around my dimples for dramatic effect.

Using the same process Claudia had demonstrated— feeling for the nexus of my left cheekbone and the muscles that meet there—I drew a razor-sharp red line, which then faded delicately, so it appeared almost airbrushed.

"Excellent! Now," she said, "the eyes! The eyes are not only the window to the soul—they are what connects you to the audience. Most of our artists do not speak, so we must magnify the eyes to show what they are feeling. Cirque is about emotion, above all!"

My character required a white base just above and below the eyes, blue eye shadow, and black eyeliner to make the eyes "pop." "We want your eyes to look *bigger* when the lights hit them," she explained.

Trusting someone enough to let them draw just millimeters from my eyes was more difficult than I would have thought, but I put my faith in Claudia's expert hand. Strange as the experience was, it was nothing compared with the bizarre feeling I had attempting the job myself on my left eye. I started blinking involuntarily, and my mouth simply refused to remain shut. "Frank," Claudia said, lightly snapping my jaw shut for me with a little tap, "we are drawing your eyes, not feeding you oats."

I laughed, and felt the muscles around my face relax. It may be difficult to learn to put your trust in another person, but it's often easier than having the confidence to trust yourself.

When I finally finished my left eye, I took a look at my work.

"Très bien, François, très bien!" I smiled into the mirror, with Claudia smiling over my shoulder. "Of course," she added, "it isn't the first time that's the problem. Artists who do it for years eventually get lazy with their makeup. We often have photos of the characters taken at the shows and sent back to us. When an artist slacks off and loses the creative spark that helped bring their character to life, you can barely recognize him or her."

I could empathize; after thirteen years doing the same

job, I had learned how to cut corners myself—and I wasn't performing before a theatre of thousands. "So how do you reignite their passion, their creativity?"

"We travel to the shows and spend a few days with them," she said. "But you can't just slap their wrists and expect them to draw better. We try to help the artists rediscover their characters. We have to be very patient and remind them that creating their characters' makeup is similar to what they do on stage: You have to keep doing the triple flip until it's so natural you can do it effortlessly, without thinking, so you will be free to focus on performing your role, portraying your character, and connecting with the audience.

"The fact that most of them were trained as athletes makes them impatient with makeup, but we've made their background work to our advantage," she said. "They are, after all, competitive. They like to be measured, to be recognized. So a few years ago I started arriving with special brushes engraved with lines like 'Best Makeup,' 'Most Improved,' 'Best Shading,' 'Best Eyes,' and so on. They love it! We want our artists to become interested in the process, because just 'following the book' is not enough. It is the difference between merely hitting the right notes on the piano and actually *playing the song*, with your whole heart, letting it flow out of you.

"We want you to make mistakes, to experiment, to discover where your personality *meets* your character's," she said. "Unlike a mask that disguises your identity, makeup helps reveal it."

Looking at my face in the mirror, I discovered that the

exaggerated, painted man staring back at me was not merely the face I'd seen flipping through the pages of Claudia's books; it was also, unmistakably, my own.

Swinging for the Fences

Cari had planned to meet several of the other performers for lunch to discuss their acts, but promised to catch up with me again later in the day. Walking through the main hallway on my way to lunch—with my makeup still on— I noticed a short man on crutches, bouncing around on his one good foot, the other trailing behind him in a neon cast. His leaps and bounds were unusually energetic for someone on crutches. Even more striking was his hair, which was coifed into two pointy, red-tinted "horns." But the infectious smile he gave me made it clear there was nothing malevolent about this devil.

"Are those real?" I asked him, pointing to the horns.

"What is 'real'?" he retorted playfully. He pointed to my painted face. "Is that real?"

I paused for a moment, then said, "Absolutely."

"Aha. Then you know why I wear my hair this way—to provoke, to excite, to have fun. When I see a hundred people with this look, I will cut the horns off, but until then, I'll keep them."

"What happened?" I asked, looking down at his crutches.

"I broke a bone in my foot. That is why I am here, building up my strength, and coaching some of the new people, instead of performing in KÀ in Las Vegas. When I was first injured, I thought, *Ohhhhhhhh no. I will be out of the show for three months.* But I've decided to make the best of it. And look, I can still move!"

He dropped his crutches and spun into a somersault. Back on his foot, he introduced himself as Martin; he was a twenty-seven-year-old acrobat from Quebec City who'd been working at Cirque for five years. "I never expected to work for Cirque," he said. "I just went to the tryouts to do some stunts and have a good time. At first, I was not very good at acrobatics. I'm a gymnast—I was trained to do gymnastic routines—so some of the craziest acrobatic stunts were new to me. But I kept at it, practicing after everyone else went home. And I tried to put my own spin on things. When a coach asked me to do a back flip, I did the craziest back flip I could imagine. And that's why I think I made the cut—I always did more than anyone expected.

"It's like your game baseball," he continued, mimicking the stance of a batter up at the plate, digging his good foot into the floor, choking up on his crutch as if it were a Louisville Slugger. "Sometimes you strike out, sometimes you hit a homer. But in life, no one cares how many times you strike out; all that matters is your home runs. And you get to bat as many times as you like! Anyone can be a home-run king if they just take enough at bats!"

What Martin was saying hit home. When had I gotten so worried about making a mistake that I'd stopped swinging for the fences? Alan used to praise my boldness—signing up an obscure college player from a second- or third-tier school who'd yet to be scouted by a professional team; or pitching advertisers on wacky new ways to feature our clients in their campaigns.

On his last swing, he whacked a large plant that stood in the corner of the hallway and sent it crashing to the floor, the dirt spilling over the sides. "See?" he said, getting on his knees to push the dirt back into the pot. "Another home run for Marty! And the crowd goes crazy!"

He was an absolute whirlwind. "What keeps you so enthusiastic about your work?" I asked.

"It all comes down to this," he said, leaning forward as if to whisper a secret. "I like challenges, I like changes, and I like to do things my own way! Because of this, I love my job. If one day I find I am no longer happy, I'll do something else. You know, we may wear these strange faces, but when we're on stage, all the makeup in the world can't cover up unhappiness. That's true in life also, isn't it? But if you're not happy, you can always do something else. You are never trapped in life. When you realize that, you find you're free to accomplish incredible things!"

Before I could respond, Marty hooked his crutch handles on his good foot, waved good-bye, and began to glide down the hallway.

On his hands.

Reinventing Yourself

Diane had set up an appointment for me to meet up with one of Cirque's new acrobatic designers who was playing a significant role in the creation of a new show. I arrived a few minutes early and bumped into him just outside his office.

"Let me guess," he said. "Claudia did the *right* side of your face."

I laughed. A young man who looked like he'd be just as comfortable riding a wave on a California beach as wading through the Montreal snow stood before me. "And why do you think that?"

"Well, the right side is sharp and clean," he said, "but your left side looks like you're seeing it through a Vaseline-covered lens, the way Ingrid Bergman looked in *Casablanca*." We both laughed. He introduced himself as Lars. Born and raised in California, he had spent years working as a production assistant in Hollywood before a friend dragged him to a Cirque du Soleil show at the Santa Monica Pier. "It was their new show's premiere in the U.S., and they had the whole city buzzing. And when I saw it, I thought, *This is the coolest thing I've ever seen*. All that energy, their wild costumes and choreography, and all the far-out acrobatics. I assumed I was too old for them—I was already twenty-eight—but I decided, *What do I have to lose?* So I made a demo tape of me tumbling on the beach, break-dancing at a club in Venice Beach, and surfing some killer waves, and sent it off to Montreal.

"They called me two weeks later. Two weeks after that, I'm in Montreal for an audition, and two weeks after *that*, I'm moving to Montreal! It was the exact opposite of my experience in Hollywood, where no one seemed to catch a break, and every supposedly new idea is just a rehash of some old movie."

Three months after sending his tape in, Lars was on a Tokyo stage for *Saltimbanco*, doing the Chinese poles and Russian swing. "But what I really loved," he said, "was the German wheel."

Seeing the puzzled look on my face, Lars explained. "The Chinese poles are poles that run from the stage floor straight up, twenty or thirty feet. You do tricks on them, jumping from one to the other, or hanging from them, horizontally, as if you were a flag. The Russian swing is this metal ramp, like the kind you use to load a moving van, only it's hanging from two metal poles and swings back and forth. You can fit three or four guys on one of those, and the guy at the front end of it gets launched, does flips in the air, and lands. Kinda dangerous, but really cool.

"The German wheel is just two big hoops connected a couple feet apart by struts. You get inside of it, hang on to the struts, all spread-eagle like *Vitruvian Man*, the drawing by Leonardo Da Vinci. Once you're in it, you can do all kinds of crazy things: You can run inside it like a gerbil in his wheel, you can do cartwheels, you can spin around like you're pivoting on your right foot. If you're really good, you can do the penny drop, where you get it on one edge and face the floor, then make it go around and around like a penny settling on the ground. But you can't let it settle all the way to the ground or you'll smash your face! So you have to be strong and balanced enough to pull out of it.

"I was dying to try it, so with the help of one of the guys in the troupe, from Germany, I ordered one. I taught myself how to do it late at night, after the *Saltimbanco* shows, screwing around on the stage after everyone had left. Man, you should have seen some of my wipeouts! I cut my shins, broke my fingers and toes, tore my ear, and broke my nose—but it was worth it!

"After a few months of training, I was good enough to

make a tape to send to Montreal. Next thing I know, I get called in to Montreal to train to be the new German wheel guy for *Quidam*. In a couple months, I'm doing *that* show!"

So many of the people I met at Cirque, it seemed, had the urge to reinvent themselves, to try new things on their own, without any assurance that their efforts would lead to anything. "Before long, I was on fire with ideas for new acrobatics, new acts, new stunts, new apparatus," Lars continued. "The atmosphere in Hollywood stifled my imagination, but the atmosphere at Cirque ignited it."

"What was the difference?"

"I don't know, maybe it's the way ideas are always crashing together here. There's so many different people from so many different backgrounds with so many cool concepts. But there's also a receptiveness to new suggestions at Cirque, too. Good ideas and good people rise to the top, regardless of seniority or politics.

"When I heard Cirque was planning to do a new show around extreme sports, I wanted to be a part of it," he added. "The casting people, who knew my background, asked me if I wanted to perform. I did, but I really wanted to sign on as a designer and develop ideas for the show. They said, 'Okay, but you better work fast. We're making decisions in a couple weeks.'

"I had a ton of ideas—too many!—but the ones I focused on were based on my experiences in California and Tokyo. When I was fifteen or so, we had an earthquake in Mendocino, maybe a six on the Richter scale. But this particular earthquake didn't shake the city back and forth, it sort of traveled along the earth's surface, rolling through the ground. I used that experience in developing some new ideas for an act.

"I made models of my best ideas out of a few hundred bucks of materials, and stayed up every night until five or six in the morning for a week, working it all out. Then I put together a fifteen-minute tape and once again sent it to Montreal. The tape made it all the way to the top of Cirque in ten days! Before I knew it, I had my own office at headquarters, and everything I needed to start trying these ideas out for real. Who knows what kind of stuff I'll dream up next? Of course, from what I hear from Diane, you'll be getting a chance to try out some of our equipment for yourself. Aren't I seeing you later today for a spin on the German wheel?"

Awakening Your Senses

Returning to my room to wash off my makeup, I tried to remember what Baudelaire said about dreams—that very few men are able to dream magnificently. Certainly, Lars was one of the few. More to the point, he had been courageous enough to follow his dreams. Despite the obstacles in his path—money, time, and resources—he never let them hold him back. He refused to think of himself as "just a performer" and worked on his own to create astonishingly original acts. It was a lesson everyone could take to heart, and it reinforced what Diane and so many at Cirque had said to me: There are no limits; anything is possible. Believe that, *live* that way, and you can accomplish extraordinary things.

My next assignment, having a plaster cast made of my head, terrified me in a way no other session had. I was to have my head and face covered in plaster for half an hour by Cirque's props technicians, who would use the cast to create a model similar to ones I remembered seeing when Diane had given me my first tour of the Cirque du Soleil headquarters.

I'd been following her down a long corridor when we passed a row of white plaster heads mounted against a wall. The clean lines of the masks had reminded me of something Michelangelo had said when asked how he created his most magnificent sculpture, *David*. "David was inside the stone—I just needed to chip away all the pieces that weren't David." Sometimes the shape of what it is we want to create already exists, I had reflected, thinking about the form of my own life and the way I wanted it to look. Maybe it was as simple as chipping away the parts of myself that no longer fit.

I had moved closer, noticing names next to each cast.

Diane had soon answered my quizzical look, "We use these plaster casts to keep track of the artists' head measurements and features."

"You mean their hat sizes?"

"Yes, something like that," she had said. "It may sound silly, but our headpieces are all custom-made for the specific roles each performer plays. Some of them are pretty elaborate, and they have to fit perfectly or they'll fall off at the wrong time—or won't come off at the right time. We found it's more convenient to keep a model of all the artists' heads here in Montreal, to fit for replacement hats, wigs, and masks rather than send out our artisans to Europe or Asia every time someone needs a new one."

Though I had certainly been impressed by the spirit of inventiveness they called upon to tackle the day-to-day problems, that did not mean I felt completely comfortable with experiencing the process firsthand. I have always been a little claustrophobic; the idea of being trapped and unable to tell anyone what I was feeling or going through was terrifying, and so it was with more than a little trepidation that I walked down to the prop shop.

I entered a space that looked like the world's most sophisticated shop class. It was filled with enormous, five-foot masks that looked like they belonged in a Mardi Gras parade. A group of men in sweaty T-shirts were sawing, molding, and painting their creations.

To my right was a small room, completely covered in white save for a peanut-butter-colored counter. In the middle stood a slender woman in a shiny yellow rubber apron. She had so much white dust on her, I first mistook her for a blonde; only later did I realize that she was a brunette in the habit of running her dusty hands through her hair. She introduced herself as Vanessa. "And this is Dolores," she said, gesturing to a cherubic and cheerful middle-aged woman behind me.

Vanessa invited me to have a seat in one of the salon-style chairs, facing a row of plaster-dusted mirrors. Clearly accustomed to working with nervous people, she explained the process to me in a calm, soothing voice. "How do you feel, Frank?" she asked. "Will you be okay with this?"

I wasn't sure that I would be, but once again, I was determined to put my trust in her hands, just as I had put my trust the day before in René's. "Yes," I said. "I'm ready."

"Okay, then, we can start," she said, and began preparing a custom-fitted latex skullcap for my head.

"Do many people have a difficult time with this?" I asked nervously.

"Oh, a few," said Vanessa as she and Dolores helped me pull on the skullcap. "You see this girl?" she said, pointing to a cast of a child's head on the countertop. "She doesn't look very comfortable, does she? Her eyes are pressed shut, hard, and her entire face is closed and tense. We had someone here speaking Chinese to her, to help her relax. We had another boy in his late teens from Brazil who asked that we let him look out while we did it. This makes it more difficult for us, but we were able to do it by making two holes for his eyes. It ended up being really funny; while we were working, his eyes kept shifting back and forth, like a painting in a spy movie. We had to work very hard not to laugh!"

I smiled at the image. But it also helped me understand a little more about *why* I was so afraid. The thought of losing my senses—even for just a few minutes—was disconcerting. Maybe it was because so much of my life depended on trying to say the right thing at the right time. The thought of having to sit still and silent, even for half an hour, unsettled me.

"Has anyone backed out halfway through?" I asked, trying hard not to betray my apprehension.

"Yes, this happens sometimes," she said, her gentle hands fitting the latex skullcap over my head. "Occasionally, a person will start to feel claustrophobic and ask to get out. But I think you will be fine."

After smoothing some lubricant over the skullcap so the plaster wouldn't stick. Vanessa and Dolores began pouring the thick concoction on my head—a surprisingly cool and comfortable sensation. Together they spread the plaster over my head, my ears, my neck, and my face.

My eyes covered, I sensed that Dolores, with her thicker, stronger fingers, was working on my right, and Vanessa, with her light delicate touch, was spreading the plaster over my forehead. I breathed through my nose while keeping my eyebrows and lips still.

The plaster was oozing over my face, and I felt as if I was slipping underwater, slowly but peacefully. As soon as I realized my head was completely covered, however, a flash flood of fear rushed through me, causing my pulse and breathing to race. I clutched the armrests. I couldn't see, I couldn't speak! But just as I thought I was about to burst, a strange thing happened. I quit fighting it, and a calm washed over me as I realized all the things I could still do.

I could still breathe. I soon accepted the rhythm of it, and I began to control it the way I'd learned to do when I first attempted the breaststroke. As I allowed my breath to become deeper, more deliberate, I found myself relaxing involuntarily. And the more I relaxed, the less compelled I felt to try to give words to what I was experiencing. It made me wonder, how often did I speak just to fill an empty moment, rather than allowing my unvoiced ideas to really take shape?

I could still smell; the minty scent of the rubberized plastic reminded me of the mouthguard molds my orthodontist used when I was a teenager. So many of my experiences at Cirque, it occurred to me, brought back strong memories, that at times it felt as if I was reliving my adolescence, with its seemingly unending series of doors leading to who knew where? Confronting these feelings, of course, often generated the same sort of awkwardness and self-consciousness I felt as a teen. The solution was not to give in to my fears, but instead work through them.

And I could still hear everything—perhaps better than before. I noticed the radio, playing what sounded like Lady Blacksmith, the group Paul Simon enlisted to play on his classic *Graceland* album. I remembered the winter I first heard the album; I was coaching swimming part-time at a private school not far from my office. I loved doing that, and yet I hadn't thought of it in years. Why had I stopped?

I recalled the way René had described how he listened for problems in the rigging. Had I become deaf to the little things that signaled what people were *really* feeling when trouble was coming? How could I open my ears and listen better?

As the minutes drifted by, I found myself in an almost meditative state. When Vanessa finally let me know it was time to remove the mold, I actually wanted them to take their time, to prolong the experience. For the first time in years, I wasn't thinking about what to say next or worrying about whether I sounded clever or smart. I was just taking it all in, savoring the sounds and smells and sensations around me.

Go with the Flow

Following my head-molding session, I headed back down to the studio, where I changed into my gym clothes and joined Lars in the middle of the floor. Cari, who knew my schedule, watched from the far wall. Lars was already playing around with the German wheel.

"Good news," he said. "You are the perfect height for the German wheel."

Being five-eight had finally paid off.

Diane had told me that she particularly wanted me to work on the German wheel, because it would show me, ultimately, how little effort was needed when my activities were performed with the right balance and timing. If you try to force your thinking down specific pathways, she explained, like the German wheel, your mind will resist you at every turn. But if you trust in your imagination, it will take you in some surprising directions.

"Show me what you can do," I asked him. Lars did not strike me as a natural show-off, but I could tell he loved to perform. He started out with a few of his simpler moves, reacclimating himself to the wheel, as it had been a while since he'd performed with it. He jammed his feet forward into the foot straps—"You want to get your shoes in there as far as you can, because if they come out, you're in big trouble"—grabbed two of the handles above, creating the *Vitruvian Man* pose, then casually tilted the wheel forward and started doing cartwheels back and forth around the floor.

He made it look effortless.

Then Lars started rolling the wheel in circles—I had no idea how he redirected the contraption, because his position didn't seem to change at all. Next he tilted it onto one edge and began spinning, the wheel getting closer and closer to the ground, the way a coin slowly settles to the floor. Even as I thought gravity would force him to fall out of the wheel and smash his face on the hardwood floor, Lars kept perfect posture. His position in the wheel never seemed to change a bit. Yet he must have been exerting some kind of force to make the wheel go where he wanted.

At the very moment it looked like he would not be able to recover from the settling spin before the wheel smacked flat on the floor, he hopped out, stood up, and gave a *Ta-da* motion, while the wheel settled into its final rotations around him. I couldn't help but clap and laugh at what I had just seen.

"That was terrific," I exclaimed.

"Just the beginning," he replied, and started spinning the hundred-pound contraption around him as easily as if it were just a six-ounce hula hoop. But it wasn't until he jumped on top of this six-foot wheel and supported himself over it using just his arms, like a gymnast mounting the parallel bars, that my jaw dropped. After holding his position for a moment— whether to establish his balance or just for dramatic effect, I didn't know—he suddenly sent his body in and out of the wheel, and over and around it, while spinning it in every possible manner. He never repeated himself, and just as I thought he'd run out of tricks, he stood *on top* of the wheel, in perfect control. "Look, Ma, no hands!" he joked.

He managed to flip himself off the wheel and jam his feet back into the foot straps, all in one motion. Keeping his arms folded in front of him, he then did another cartwheel, using only his feet! Back and forth, around and around, he repeated several of the moves he'd demonstrated minutes earlier, but this time with no arms to assist him.

But there was one thing he couldn't do without his arms, I was sure: the penny drop. At that moment, he grabbed the handle above with one hand—and did the penny drop! As his body, and the wheel, came closer and closer to being horizontal with the floor, the wheel began rocking like a whirling dervish. Finally, Lars got the wheel spinning so fast, I couldn't follow his head without getting dizzy—he had transformed himself into a human gyroscope!

And when I thought there was no escaping this time— there he was, standing up in the middle of the wheel as the wheel finished spinning around him. No need for a *ta-da* this time. The whole act spoke for itself.

I was awed to the point of silence. And I was a little scared. After all, it was my turn next.

"Look, it's not that hard," he said, urging me to come forward. But I had seen too many things already that, in the hands of a world-class performer, looked easy but proved very difficult in the hands of an amateur. Like, say, me. And this list was constantly growing.

"Trust me," Lars said, seeing the doubt on my face.

"Once you get the balance, you're all set. The key is, you can't fight the wheel, you must work with it. You change direction not by yanking it this way or that—it'll resist you—but with subtle manipulations."

"All right," I said, jamming my feet as far as I could into the straps and grabbing the handles.

"Oh yeah," he said, as if he'd just thought of this. "The main thing is NEVER let go. If you're going to crash, just crash—you're safer in the wheel than outside it. Because if your hands or feet are outside the wheel when you crash, you'll break your fingers and toes."

I just shot him a look.

But I was up for it. I'd survived all the challenges I had faced so far. Once I got myself situated in the wheel, I started rocking back and forth, just to get a feel for it.

"Another tip," he said. By now I felt like a sucker at a car dealership, getting stuffed with tack-on after tack-on. "You need to keep your body as rigid as you can, as flat as you can. The more you focus on your 'core strength'—your stomach and chest—the more control you'll have."

Before long, however, I felt surprisingly safe inside the wheel; I did a few cartwheels down the floor, then did them back the other way.

"Good," he said. "Now try walking inside the wheel."

If you can imagine a human attempting to emulate a gerbil in a Habitrail, you know what I looked like. At first, however, I was so tentative, so mistrusting of my ability, that the wheel barely moved, even as I seemed to be straining every muscle in my body.

"Like I said," Lars instructed, "you're going to have to trust this thing, and yourself. Most of the things you do on the wheel are actually easier the faster you're going. The wheel is easier to control, easier to adjust, with a little speed. And you're going to tire yourself out, your way."

I took another step inside the wheel, but this time didn't try to hold back, instead leaning forward, letting the wheel do its thing. As Lars cheered me on, I started rolling the big white wheel down the floor . . . and right into the big white concrete wall at the end of it. I braced for the crash, held on tight—and found it wasn't that bad! I had gotten thrown back on my butt—fortunately, my least vulnerable attribute.

"There you go!" Lars said.

"But didn't you see me crash?" I asked, picking myself up.

"That's why I'm clapping!" he said. "If you don't learn how to crash correctly, you're not going to learn anything else about the German wheel. When you're starting out, it's *mostly* crashes. Man, you should have seen some of the killers I had on the *Saltimbanco* stage, working with the wheel. I rolled that sucker five, six rows into the stands more times than I'd like to count. But once I learned how to brace myself and stay inside it, I was okay. And I quit being afraid of screwing up. That's when it becomes fun!"

I got back in the wheel, started rolling around again, and discovered—he was right! Instead of fearing the next wall in front of me, I just started experimenting with how I could make the wheel do what I wanted, within the rules that governed it. Lean a bit to the inside, and I could get it on one rail. Lean forward, I could make it speed up; lean back, and I could make it slow down and even reverse itself.

"Now," Lars said, "it's time for you to go three-sixty. Once you know how to pivot completely inside the wheel, there's no place you can't go."

Lars showed me a series of complicated maneuvers with my hands and feet—grabbing a rail behind me here, some fancy footwork there—all designed to get my body turned around within the wheel while it was rolling, without getting tangled up or off balance.

It was slow going at first, but once I started to sense the balance points and work with them, suddenly I began to move gracefully in the middle of the wheel, even as it was rolling smoothly down the floor.

"That's it, that's it!" Lars said. "Don't fight it! If you work with it, it'll work with you. Now you're doing it! You can muscle it everywhere, but it's far better to learn to flow with the wheel and use it to your advantage."

After just a short while, there I was, walking forward, walking backward, doing cartwheels, making the wheel turn this way and that—and doing all of those things while I turned around inside it. It wasn't mastery over the wheel, of course. I was months or years from that, if I was lucky. But it did represent mastery over my old way of thinking, of facing an uncooperative element with brute force. By approaching the wheel with patience and trust, and being attuned to its balance point, I found myself working with it, not against it.

It was exactly what Diane wanted me to learn. You have to be confident enough to let your imagination spin off in all kinds of directions. And if you really want to make things happen, you have to be willing to crash.

chapter six

The Lights of Paris

Leaving Your Comfort Zone

As our plane approached Charles de Gaulle Airport, I looked out onto the magical lights of the Paris skyline below. I had been invited to the Paris debut of one of Cirque's oldest shows, *Saltimbanco*. I was traveling with Cari, who was spending several weeks in the City of Lights to learn the art of the double trapeze from the Brazilian twins performing the act in the show. Understandably, she was nervous; unable to sleep, she had spent the last several hours going over the information packet on Paris that Cirque had prepared for her.

Diane had wanted me to get an inside look at the "traveling village"—her name for the touring shows. She felt I

could not fully understand what Cirque was about until I'd
seen life on the road. And there was no better time to
experience that aspect of life at Cirque than at a premiere
in a new city. Raising the Grand Chapiteau in a new mar-
ket, she explained, is a ceremony at Cirque.

Having spent the last three weeks in the Studio experiencing Cirque's culture, she told me, it was crucial that I
see how all the aspects of training and preparation, design
and creation, coordination and cooperation are integrated
into the daily life of a show. "The Studio is a mesmerizing
wonderland, a place where our artists learn to set free the
reins of their imagination," she said. "But eventually, they
all must leave the safety of the Studio's walls and experience the sometimes brutal reality of performing 375 times
a year. Seeing one of our touring shows—especially *Saltimbanco*—will allow you to witness the incredible exchange
of emotional energy which takes place between the performer and the spectator."

"Why *Saltimbanco*?" I had asked.

"It is our longest-running show, but it is also incredibly
fresh," she explained. "To keep any show running, we have
to question whether it still fits in an ever-changing world.
Before we choose to send a show to a new city or country,
we ask, 'Is it relevant? Is it stimulating?' Our creative
directors believe that *Saltimbanco* still meets all those cri-
teria, which is why we began touring the show once again
after its original run ended in 1997.

"And in a sense, *Saltimbanco* is a microcosm of Cirque
du Soleil itself. When the show was being conceived, the
creators started with the theme of the urban experience—

many cultures swirling together into a colorful blend of personalities, stories, and music. Traveling from city to city is an essential part of circus life. Often, it's when our creators leave behind the comfort of home that they come up with their most intriguing ideas."

After having met with a small sampling of the 3,000 employees and artists from over forty different countries who called the Montreal Studio home, I was eager to see how all their efforts came together to create one show, one performance. Over the past few weeks, I'd met any number of Cirque du Soleil "guides," as Diane called them—scores of performers, creative and artistic directors, a sampling of the hundreds of artisans, technicians, front-of-house employees, and head-office professionals who helped to orchestrate Cirque's many ventures. I had trained for weeks with Igor on developing the basic physical skills required to perform acrobatic routines, and Lars and Tatiana had taught me some of the secrets of the German wheel and bungee-trapeze. I had met with chefs and licensing people, attorneys and interpreters, wig and costume makers. Together, they had opened my mind to such an extent that I knew I would not be seeing *Saltimbanco* with the same eyes that had taken in KÀ in Las Vegas months before.

In some ways, I wasn't the same *person* I was before coming to Cirque. Something inside me had changed; no longer did I feel like the world around me was just a steady, monotonous continuum, each day as predictable as the next. Through my conversations and experiences, I'd gradually come to see that each day was alive with possibilities. I felt a renewed sense of excitement at what I could make of my life.

I started to question even the most basic things I had always taken for granted. I wore a suit to work every day. Why? I could easily toss out my old suits and wear what I wanted for a change. I could change the way I interacted with my colleagues and clients. I could reinvent my job— whether or not I changed my profession or career. These feelings left me energized, as well. It was a subtle shift in perspective, but a real one, as if my flat, black-and-white world had suddenly become a colorful, three-dimensional landscape.

My experience reminded me of something Diane had told me about one of their shows, *Quidam*. The story follows an adolescent girl who is somewhat disillusioned by the world around her. Her father, clad in a Magritte-inspired suit and bowler, travels to work each day in a line of other businesspeople sleepwalking through life. Her mother stares blindly ahead, seeing nothing. The girl, bored yet curious, longs for the kind of excitement she believes lies just beyond her reach, and as a result, dreams up the magical Quidam, a headless, umbrella-carrying being. With his help, she learns that all it takes to transform the ordinary world into an extraordinary adventure is a little imagination.

And, of course, the right guides. I'd learned so much from Diane, Igor, and the others about opening myself up to the creative stimuli around me. And about risk-taking— not just the big risks, but the small chances you take every day that give your life a sense of excitement, of possibility.

I'd been taught the secret of trust—trusting your friends, your colleagues, yourself. It was so much clearer to me what a powerful force real teamwork and collaboration could be. Nothing seemed more crucial to creating and nurturing new ideas.

A trapeze artist could never take flight without the expert work of her riggers and coaches; a contortionist could never help the audience embark on a journey into the imagination were it not for the makeup artists and costume designers who brought her character and performance together in colorful union. Each act, each movement, each moment was the culmination of the efforts of a cast of hundreds.

Cari and I arrived at the Cirque site the next morning. Located on the huge parking lot of a former Renault factory, the grounds were bustling with activity and the ebullient energy to which Diane had alluded. Riggers with huge squeegees rappelled from the apex of the big top, washing down the vinyl panels, restoring them from the gray grime of the road to the pure white of a new beginning. Other crew members were setting up concession stands and souvenir displays. Several technicians were rolling in racks of assorted costumes, their colors as wild and varied as a rain-forest canopy. I felt as if we had stepped into a Technicolor version of an Amish barn-raising—workers performing their tasks in a carefully choreographed dance.

Cari and I walked past the big top and the first of two

small tops—which served as the lobby—and toward the second small top, the artists' "backstage" area. While a boom box played the Grateful Dead's "Touch of Gray," I watched the artists warming up, stretching, juggling balls, testing themselves on the high wire and Chinese poles. There was a strongman sitting shirtless on a trunk, lifting a dumbbell over his head, talking to a fellow performer. With a handlebar mustache, he could have been transported whole cloth from a nineteenth-century American circus.

I asked a woman mounting a bicycle where I might find Maurice Morenz, the artistic director of the show. She pointed to a man in a red-and-white-striped shirt, standing outside a trailer that served as the company kitchen—*la cantine* in French. "Maurie-Mo!" she said. "You have visitors!"

"Bienvenue, mon ami!" he said. Moments later, he was shaking my hand and giving Cari the typical French Canadian kiss on both cheeks. Maurice gave Cari directions on where she could find her new coach, then he invited me to join him for a cup of coffee.

Diane had told me this was Cirque's first show in Paris in sixteen years. When I asked Maurice how he felt, he acknowledged that he was nervous.

"Paris is one of the last big world capitals we have to conquer, and the pressure is great. They have a rich circus tradition here, going back centuries. If we have a good premiere, if they are open to what Cirque is about, then I think we'll be fine. Of course, if we don't catch on immediately, it could be a very long and lonely three months."

I told Maurice I found his anxiety surprising given the history of the show and the experience of the performers. He said, "*Au contraire*, my friend! We face our fears every day. The fact is, we WANT to scare ourselves some—to reach our limits and then go beyond them. We have to shove ourselves off the cliff before we start flying. The greatest danger is not failing but getting comfortable, of reaching a certain altitude and putting the show on auto-pilot. And Paris is a perfect place for us to embrace discomfort. With the exception, perhaps, of New York, I can't think of another city where the artistic expectations are so high."

"So how do you avoid getting too comfortable?"

"We like to mix the performers up with artistic groups we encounter in our travels—jugglers, acrobats, fire-breathers, musicians, mimes, puppeteers, circus schools, dance groups, even a cabaret. We encounter artistic groups in every city that we visit. If they offer something special, as has often been the case in Europe, we might invite them in to do a workshop for our artists—it's part of keeping our artists 'challenged' and fresh. Or we might organize an exchange—we do a workshop for them and they do one for us. Or we invite them to one of our shows. When we were creating KÀ, we worked with a French group we'd discovered called 'Les Yamakazi." They helped us to develop the act that featured artists leaping from one giant pillar to another; the group also influenced the style of climbing along the catwalks that stretch above the audience. It just goes to show, you never know where such a chance encounter will lead!"

No one knew this better than me; after all, my entire journey had been set in motion by my chance encounter with Diane. Was there a way, I wondered, to ensure I'd be more receptive to such serendipity in the future? Part of me already knew the answer was yes: by overcoming my fears, by learning to trust others and share my ideas, by taking risks.

Maurice waved me into the company kitchen. It was decorated with colorful tables painted by the people who'd toured with the troupe over the years—the artists, support staff, and their children—depicting maps of their hometowns, from Kansas to Kazakhstan. We walked over to a counter filled with an array of fine coffees and teas.

Looking around, Maurice said, "I have become convinced that the more we nourish our artists and support staff—in every way—the more they'll give back in return. Our goal is to make the artists comfortable in just about every way possible, so we can make them *uncomfortable* in their thinking—challenge them, destabilize them. The more we do that, the more they'll throw themselves into their roles. When the performers first join a touring show, they're like guests at a thrilling party—traveling the world, meeting new people, seeing new cities. But after a while, the smart ones realize their bodies are tools that need to be honed and treated with care. They realize their roles are only the starting point—it's what they put into their characters that makes the difference. It's like playing Hamlet. The role's already been performed a thousand times. But did Laurence Olivier play the role the same way Kenneth Branagh did?"

Working with What You Have

As I entered the big top, one of the trapeze artists, Valesca, was showing Cari how to adjust her grip on the trapeze bar. I introduced myself to their coach, Johann. As we watched them, he explained to me that he wasn't testing Cari's trapeze skills—it was too early for that. "This is not natural for Cari," he said as they practiced a few basic swings and transitions. "Our first step is to let her learn to trust the trapeze and her partner. Competing as a gymnast, she's never had to do that before."

Cari gripped the hands of the other twin, Julia, who dangled from the trapeze by her knees and then began swinging Cari so that she could get the feel of the movement.

"We do a lot of repetition in practice until everything becomes second nature," Johann explained.

"Once we get the basics down, the ideas start flowing. Valesca and Julia are particularly ambitious—the kind of artists I love to work with. They want their act to go somewhere, so they push themselves. In the two years I've worked with them, we've made major changes at least a half-dozen times. And they're the ones who proposed the changes, which makes my job easy.

"Of course, sometimes they have good ideas they haven't thought all the way through. Instead of telling them why it won't work, I say, 'Let's see how we can work with this.' You can't simply say, 'No, that will not work,' or they will quit pushing themselves. To remain motivated, they have to feel their ideas and input are taken seriously.

"We want artists who are willing to take their acts to the next level. If your attitude is 'I'm doing my job,' then you're really not doing your job. The audience is paying for more than that. They want to feel the *inspiration*.

"A big part of my job is figuring out how to handle each artist—and it can change every hour! Just a few months ago, I took one of our young artists aside because I thought he needed a little advice. He was beginning to behave like a prima donna—yelling at this person, complaining about that, pouting and whining. Usually, I let the young performers find their way. But this time I had had enough. I sat him down and said, 'What were you doing before you came to Cirque? And what will you be doing if you lose this job?' I told him to stop complaining and start enjoying himself. He was a little stunned—no one had ever challenged him to rethink his behavior before. But he got the message. Since then, I've seen a tremendous shift in his attitude.

"The show, too, is always changing. People leave, people join us, performers get injured—sometimes in the middle of a show. You have to figure out how to make it all work with what you have. It's a big puzzle every night. But I suppose the same is true no matter what you do. The secret is having people who can deliver something special when resources are limited."

Johann turned his attention back to the trapeze, where Cari swung from the trapeze bar into Valesca's outstretched hands without the slightest hesitation. Valesca caught her and, after gliding through the air for a moment, let go, just as Cari made her graceful landing. "That's it, Cari. Beautiful!"

Creating a Community

Later that afternoon, I caught up with one of the Cirque clowns Diane had wanted me to meet, Philippe. Philippe, she had felt, could explain better than anyone what it was like to interact with the audiences and make them part of the creative experience.

When I arrived at his dressing room, Philippe was putting on his makeup, a white base with intense black eyebrows. Wearing black shoes and white socks, baggy black shorts and suspenders, a bow tie and red cap, he looked like an overgrown schoolboy.

In fact, he told me he was thirty-five, although he looked no older than twenty. The role was perfect for him—especially with his boyish face, physique, and demeanor—even though he was at least the fifth man to play it. He took his time applying his makeup, trying out a range of facial expressions until he was satisfied.

"If people realize I'm thirty-five," he said, "they won't allow their imaginations to run wild. They'll see me as an adult acting, rather than a kid playing. Most people in the audience want to forget the rules, but they need a little help. I have to create an imaginary world for them: If I do it well, they will walk into it with me."

Philippe had been performing his role in *Saltimbanco* for the last two years. "I took over the role from another clown named Pascal. At first I just mimicked him, but eventually my own personality took over. He was more cynical than I am, a little more confrontational with the audience, where I'm clearly a boyish buffoon, on the audience's side. That works better for me. I have to be a happy character or it's not fun.

"When I pull someone from the audience onto the stage prior to the start of a show, my goal is to give that individual, and the audience, a taste of this rich, imaginary world that this child I play lives in. For most of us, it's been too long since we've played like children! And I insist, very nicely but firmly, that they follow the rules of my make-believe world. I want the people I pick to have fun, too. I want them to be the heroes in my piece. I'll whisper to them: 'Can you help me?' And they usually do. But for this to happen, you have to establish trust with them—lots of trust." In my time at Cirque, I'd realized trust was something of a mantra.

Philippe continued, "There also has to be a feeling of spontaneity—that what the audience will see tonight will not be the same tomorrow night. That it is just for them. That is the beauty of this act.

"To come across as sincere on the stage, you must be sincere in life. It's important for the audience to feel that we're all together as a community, with a shared sense of beauty, of joy. When I feel this, everything else seems to fall into place."

Attention to Details

Diane had jumped through hoops to set up a meeting for me with the man who caught fire in "O," as it was his image that had inspired me to take a deeper look inside Cirque du Soleil. Murray was in Paris for the *Saltimbanco* premiere and to explore new ideas for his own act. I met him in the big top, watching the performers rehearse. My first question was the obvious one: "Do you ever get burned during the show?"

"I've been doing this for twenty-five years, so you can't avoid getting burned at some point. Plumbers get wet, beekeepers get stung every once in a while. I use the best materials I can, the right fuels and clothes and stunt gels. But even with those things, it's dangerous. The world record for being on fire is two minutes and thirty seconds, and I burn for two minutes and fifteen seconds every night. We time it to the exact second, because you can only go so long before the materials break down."

"Does the time you're on fire on stage go by in a blur?"

"Actually, quite the opposite," Murray said. "Everything is more drawn out on stage; everything seems longer. A few seconds seem like a minute—not just to me, but to you too. I take my time, shuffling along, which creates the illusion that I've been burning for a long time, when it isn't *that* long. The rest of the troupe does a great job of distracting the audience with all this fast stuff, which helps to cloud their perception of time. It seems agonizing—to you!"

When I asked Murray how he got started, he said he began working with fire when he was eighteen. He started traveling with his own show, then joined other circuses, and one day he got the call to come on David Letterman's show.

"I sent him a tape of me juggling fire. They called and said, 'What else do you have?' 'Well,' I told them, 'I can juggle and jump a rope in flames on a unicycle.' 'Okay,' they said, 'anything else?'

"I had started to design a new trick where I'm shackled, and I jump into a big cattle tub full of water, with gasoline on top, blazing. They said, 'Yeah, that's what we want!' The only problem was, I had never done it—and the show was in one week! I told them I would bring all the stuff for it, but if I couldn't do it safely, I would have to back out. So the first time I did it live was on *Letterman*. When I got out of the tub, my hair caught fire just for a second—a great visual! Letterman loved it. He pretty much gave me an open invitation. Whenever I come up with something new, they have me back on. I've been on five or six times.

"Afterward, all the agents who said fire is a dead end started calling me up and telling me how great I was."

"You must enjoy flirting with disaster," I said.

"Far from it!" he said. "I'll take a little risk with fire, but not a big one. Only a fool does that. People think I'm a wild and crazy guy who'll do anything—and that couldn't be further from the truth. When I'm working, I like to control everything I do; any change in the environment can make a big difference in how the fire behaves. If someone does something as simple as opening a door backstage, a funny little act can become pretty terrifying pretty fast.

"One time I was going to appear on a local TV show and they had just waxed the floor. I asked if it was okay to do my act, and they said sure—and, of course, during my rehearsal the floor catches on fire and I'm going crazy trying to put it out. I had to do the show later that day sooo carefully, knowing that if anything touched that floor, we'd all go up in flames.

"I've learned to pay a lot of attention to detail—first of

all, because my life depends on it, but also because doing so means every night will be a little different. One night I'm looking at how the fire responds when I move my right arm. Another night I'm watching how differently it is coming off the newspaper than off of my shoes. No matter what happens, every night I'm alive to it."

Flexibility

It was dark as I made my way out of the big top. Knowing how determined Diane was to have me meet Murray, I reflected on what he'd told me. He'd made a convincing argument for the importance of controlling your environment and paying attention to details. But I couldn't help wondering if something else he'd said was even more important. Before I could sort out my thoughts, however, I heard someone yell, "Frank!" from the parking lot. It was Maurice waving me toward his car. "Some of us are going down the street for a drink—there's a place we've been going to unwind. Care to join us?"

I climbed into Maurice's car; he drove a couple blocks to a nondescript brick box that looked more like a storage facility than a bar. There were no windows, or even a sign identifying the place by name. The door of the entrance blended in so well with the brick that if you didn't have a guide, you'd never find it.

Inside, I heard the sultry voice of a Parisian chanteuse, which mingled with the laughter and many dialects of the Cirque employees. "Ah, here are two people you must meet," Maurice said, and, whisking me over to the bar, introduced me to Eman, a stocky Asian man with long, black muttonchops, and Wally, a tall redhead who spoke with a New Zealand accent. When another group of people waved him over to their table, Maurice excused himself politely.

"You know," I said to Eman, "you kind of look like—"

"An Asian Elvis," he said. "I know."

"He gets that all the time," Wally said. "In fact, I think he kind of likes it, or he'd change that awful hairdo. I'm Wally. Are you new to Cirque?"

"Sort of," I said. "I've been going through training in Montreal. But I'm a sports agent from Chicago; one of my clients just came on board a few weeks ago. Diane McKee felt that immersing myself in the experience of Cirque might help me introduce new athletes to the company. So I'm here finding out what the touring life is like. What do you do?"

"I make costumes," Wally said, "and Eman is an artistic director and something of a jack-of-all-trades. Of course, trying to explain exactly what any of us do is a bit tricky. As Mark Twain said: Analyzing humor is like trying to dissect a frog. You can do it, but the frog tends to die in the process. A lot of what we do is simply hard work. If you wait for your muse to arrive to give you inspiration, you can wait all day and have nothing to show for it. Al Hirschfeld, the cartoonist, put it like this: 'Everybody is creative, and everybody is talented. I just don't think everybody is disciplined.'"

"Diane mentioned that you come up with some of your greatest ideas on the road," I said.

"Sometimes, yes," said Eman. "We came to Paris not only to see the premiere of *Saltimbanco*, but also to soak up the artistic energy in the City of Lights."

"Our costume designer for 'O,' our Las Vegas water show, went to Venice for inspiration," Wally added. "She wanted to see how water reflected the cycles of life. That became a main theme of the show."

"What else inspires you?" I asked, curious.

"Problems," Wally said. "When it's too easy, I get bored. If there are no problems, I do the expected instead of something *exciting.*"

"When I think of problems, I think of 'O'!" Eman said, rolling his Elvis eyes.

"None of our shows presented us with more complications," Wally agreed. "Then again, we say that *every* time! We're always pushing the envelope, always trying something new, something audacious. You cannot do things on a new show the way you did them before. But with 'O,' this was especially true, because it was our first water show."

"Of course, we didn't want that challenge to stop us from what we wanted to do," Eman said. "We didn't want the water to be heavy, we wanted it to be light, to be fun, to be *flexible.* You see the show, and you see people diving in it, jumping out of it, even walking on it! But we had to experiment a lot to make all of that happen."

"Let me give you an example from my own work," Wally said. "The creators wanted these exotic costumes with exotic colors. But the costumes get dunked twice a night in chlorinated water. We had to find new materials, new dyes, new waterproof makeup to make it all work in water. Just about everything we did on that show started with a conversation with someone outside of our department. The coach wanted something that fit loose, even when wet, and the director wanted one costume that looked like a zebra, another that looked like a moon. Whatever it was, we had to come up with it. But I love that! The worst thing someone can do to me is give me a blank white page and say, 'Create something.' I'm not a designer, I'm a cutter. I love to take other people's ideas and run with them, push them, give them more than they expect. I don't understand people who say, 'It's not my job to be creative.' Well, then, you're selling your job short!"

"Your job is what you make it," Eman jumped in. "We have a woman who has worked here at Cirque for five years as a receptionist. But she was also a musician. And when a show was being developed that needed specialized classical instruments, she auditioned for it and won the part! Now she's a member of our touring company."

"Cirque attracts the kind of people who go beyond what's expected of them," Wally said. "And for the costumes in 'O,' our team needed to develop new materials that dried faster, stretched more, and held their colors longer. But they also needed to look sheerer, more elastic than any fabric we'd ever seen—more like the skin of a seal or otter than something man-made. We didn't try to adapt our existing costumes to the water; instead, we created something new, something better!

"You've heard of Buckminster Fuller?" Wally asked me, seemingly out of the blue.

"Don't you know any Asian philosophers?" Eman chided.

Wally laughed. "Fuller said when he started to design something to solve a problem, he was not trying to make something beautiful. But if his final solution was not beautiful, he knew he had missed something. It's the same for us. We start out just trying to avoid disaster. But in the end, if we don't come up with something special, we know we need to think some more. Our costumes for 'O' came about because we were trying to solve a problem."

"We really didn't know anything about working with water before we started 'O,'" Eman remembered. "It made us humble. We had to start from zero."

"Every show seems to present its own challenges," Wally said. "On *Varekai*, the director wanted one of our central characters to be dressed in a tube, which evolves into a caterpillar; he wanted us to design the costume with spiky sleeves. But he didn't take into account that our artists have to move—a lot! So I had two challenges—make spiky sleeves, but make them really flexible.

"I started with stretchy mesh, see-through, then added some plastic pieces to create the spiky arms. My first attempt was a nightmare—way too clumsy; it made it impossible for the artist to perform her act. The second one looked like an Asian dragon! But one night, as I was obsessing about this, I went to bed and it just popped into my head. I would add wings with plastic boning in them, so they can expand and transform the performer without interfering with her movements. It was fluid, flexible, and strong all at once.

"The next day, I went to work a little early to get started. I wanted to work it out myself to see if it would fly. I tried a small model first and saw that, yeah, it was going to work.

"So I made a full-scale model and showed it to Tai, a colleague. She thought my model was cool but not quite there yet. So we started brainstorming ideas, anticipating problems—that one's too hard to make, that one's going to tear, that one won't last long enough. Right away, sparks start flying. Sometimes Tai and I come at things from different perspectives. In fact, Cirque purposely teams up people from different backgrounds with different personalities, in the hopes that we'll come up with something more original. Working with a teammate like Tai, I know I'm not in it by myself. And together, we came up with the right solution."

Learning to Trust

When I arrived at the Cirque site the next evening, the performers were a little anxious. In the artistic tent, the artists were stretching, quietly rehearsing their routines, and applying their makeup.

As the show began, I was struck by the music, a fusion of vastly different styles, from Argentine drumming to opera. Johann had told me about it the day before. "When creating the music, the composer found it challenging to bring the theme of urban life to the score. So he imagined what it would sound like if he drove his car through a city like New York with the windows rolled down; he would hear everything from rock to African to classical music. And that's what he tried to capture, the diverse sounds of urban life in a cosmopolitan city."

When the drums changed tempo, the first act began. I'd seen the first three performers—a man, woman, and child—rehearsing the day before. The little boy was the son of two adult performers. "When he was very small," Johann had told me, "he asked his mother, 'Why is everyone working except me?'"

As the family's act came to a dramatic close, the father was gently swinging his son, whose arms and legs were twisted into a pretzel, into wide arching loops above his head. As they left center stage, Philippe the clown skipped over to take their place. He soon picked a man out of the stands and coaxed him through an imaginary door. The man obliged, crawling through the invisible square Philippe had traced in the air and leaving his old world behind.

After Philippe bounced off stage, he went off to check his makeup. A few minutes later, he came over to me, waving hello. I congratulated him on the audience's wild applause.

"Thank you," Philippe said. "Of course, they were responding to the man I plucked from the audience, not me. They're not really cheering his ability but his courage in letting himself go and trusting me, in front of all those people. Really, he did what all of us must do to be creative, to be alive: He let his guard down and jumped in!"

"How do you pick your volunteers?" I asked.

"Good question," he said. "It is not random. I wear a different costume and a mask for the opening of the show. As

I'm walking through the crowd, I try to read the people. This job teaches you the importance of paying attention to body language.

"If I want to play it safe, I pick a guy who looks friendly but shy, and he will almost always play along. But if I want to take a chance, I might pick a bigger guy, stronger, someone with a beard who sits with his arms folded, keeping the world at bay. Right now I feel strong, like I want to take that kind of risk."

"What if he doesn't play along?"

Philippe grinned at me and said, "We'll see!"

With that, Philippe clapped his hands and jumped up to open the second act. He walked around the aisles, listening to the crowd respond as he slowed down before this person or that, giving the impression he was going to bring each of them to the stage. Philippe finally came to a complete stop in front of a hefty guy in his fifties, and gave him a solicitous look. The crowd responded with hearty laughter, but you could tell they sensed trouble in the man's stern face. Undeterred, Philippe gestured for the man to stand up. Then he tried to engage him in simple hand play—hand shakes and high fives.

But the man's arms remained folded, his brow furrowed, resisting Philippe's every overture. Instead of appearing put off, Philippe gestured to the audience to give the man a nice round of applause, and gave him a kidlike hug.

Soon enough, Philippe found another volunteer. This time, the audience member gleefully spun the imaginary pistol Philippe had given him. From there, the two rolled into a goofy Western shoot-out. Looking around, I saw that it wasn't only the children who were enjoying the act; everyone in the audience was smiling—even Philippe's first unwilling assistant.

After Philippe left the stage, *Saltimbanco* began its final crescendo. The singer, in her plumed headdress and sparkling gown, voiced the show's operatic aria, and four bungee-trapeze artists, in costumes as white as doves, took center stage. While they twirled and soared through the air in a serene dance, my eyes alternated between their aerial feats and the legion of wild dancing creatures below them. *Saltimbanco*, I realized, was not one story but many. At any given moment of the performance, by looking away from the center of the ocean, I would see an altogether different tale. In that way, it mirrored what I'd experienced at Cirque. Each person I'd met was but a quarter note in a grand symphony, but each was absolutely essential.

After the show reached its climactic conclusion, the entire troupe came out to take a bow, basking in a well-earned standing ovation. The performers then took their masks off, an emotional moment that allowed the audience to connect with them on another level.

"I love it when we come out for the encore," Philippe said to me as he and the other artists filed backstage. "When we pull off our masks and hats, we reveal our souls, our humanity; we're showing the audience that, really, we're just like you. If we can do this, you can, too."

"I'm sorry that first guy you approached was so difficult," I said, referring to his performance in the second act.

"Don't be," he said. "That first man made the night special. He let the audience know the show is real, that it's not all contrived, that we are taking chances. People like that. When the little-boy clown hugs the big guy, and moves on sadly to another volunteer, and then perks up—that's beautiful! That is life!

"It's never my failures that I regret, it's the things I pass up because I'm too scared, too safe. There's a lesson in that that the audience can take away. The first man would not trust me. He essentially told me, 'Don't make a fool of me.' But I was not trying to make a fool of him. I was trying to make a fool out *of me*—I just needed his help. The second man, though, overcame his fears; he did not worry about what people thought, and instead he trusted me. And he became a hero.

"If you want to live fully," Philippe said with a smile, "you have to trust."

The next day, I was back at Charles de Gaulle Airport, ready to return to Chicago. My Cirque adventure was coming to an end. As a result of all I'd seen, heard, and experienced, I felt confident that I would live my life more creatively. But I knew Diane hadn't just wanted me to approach my job with a different attitude, another set of tools. She wanted to inspire me to think of my work as a calling once again. As I waited in line to have my bags checked by airport security, I thought back to something Diane had told me one of the designers had said he'd kept in mind when conceiving *Quidam*, a show whose set suggests a train station. "You take one train or another, you can change your life's direction." And then the reason Diane

had been so anxious for me to talk to Murray, the fire performer, became clear. Only after he appeared on television
did the agents knock down his doors. If they'd been more
open to taking on new clients *before* they were front page
news, they'd have had a much better chance of represent-
ing him. Had I fallen into the same pattern? Had I lost my
ability to spot talented athletes before they made it big?

I knew now what I had to do to get my passion back,
to regain that creative spark. It was simply a matter of
remembering where my journey began.

Finding the Pearl Within

Coaching

Several months later, I found myself back in Las Vegas once again. Cari had been asked to fill in for several weeks for one of the characters in KÀ, and I had come to watch her debut.

My first night in Las Vegas, the night before Cari's debut, I received a ticket from Diane for *Mystère*, the first of Cirque's resident shows in Vegas. As I strolled up the carpeted walkway to the concourse of the theatre, I was met by an older man eager to look at my ticket. He looked like an eccentric, mad scientist, with black high-tops, black dress pants, a dress shirt, and black sport coat, his salt-and-pepper hair fried out to the sides. He made a big show of leading me to my seat. After he sat me down, he surprised the woman sitting next to me by whisking her away on his arm. The crowd howled.

She had become part of the show.

Those of us in the audience watched the clownish usher continue his antics. After examining one couple's tickets, he had the man hold his flashlight, then tore up the tickets in their faces; he led others on a wild-goose chase over the seats themselves, instead of through the aisles; he bumped another man from his seat and sat down in his place; and he escorted unsuspecting guests on serpentine tours of the entire theatre, before finally depositing them in the farthest possible seat from where they started. He repeatedly spilled popcorn on himself and on patrons in every row.

He got big laughs for his stunts, of course—but more important, he was creating a bond with the audience, making them part of an inside joke, breaking down the barriers between artists and spectators, even before the performance started. Diane had told me, months before, how crucial this clown character was to the story of *Mystère*. The mischievous and somewhat cantankerous usher was a kind of Charon, forever stuck in limbo between the real world and the one on stage. To truly enter the world of the imagination, you must first humor these tricksters, but ultimately, you must find your own way in.

The show itself was, not surprisingly, mesmerizing, all the more so, since I'd practiced some of the stunts myself. As six performers spun around the bungee-trapeze like phoenixes in flight, I felt as if I were reliving a dream.

After the show, I took a cab to the Bellagio Hotel to meet up with Diane, who was in Vegas developing a new act. She and some of the other Cirque performers had gathered in a lounge at the 'O' theatre after the evening's first show.

After I entered the room, Diane and I gave each other a huge hug. Her eyes were dancing with energy; she seemed to feed off the electricity in the room. But what surprised me was how delighted she seemed to see me; something in my own eyes had obviously caught her attention, and she'd liked what she'd seen.

"You look so aware, so caught up in everything around you," she said. "And you've lost weight, haven't you?"

"Well, you look radiant yourself," I replied, taking her hands. "And you're right. I have lost weight. In general, I just feel so much more engaged these days. Thanks to you," I said, lowering my head slightly in appreciation. "It was you who made all that happen, who opened all those doors for me at Cirque."

"Perhaps, yes. But the journey, the hard work you put in—that was all you. I'm glad I could help open a few doors. But you've seen Philippe's act in *Saltimbanco*. He might draw the door in the air, but unless the audience member has the courage to step through, Philippe might as well have drawn a brick wall," she said. "And you don't have to thank me. It's enough of a reward to see you living up to your potential."

My life had changed in countless ways, large and small, since I'd first walked through the seven doors at the KÀ theatre. I was still living in Chicago, still working at the agency, but that's where the similarities between my old life and my new life ended. When I'd returned, refreshed, Alan offered me the opportunity to take on our two biggest clients, last year's Heismann trophy winner, and the point guard of the NBA team favored to win the play-offs this year. Alan wanted me to have a larger share in the firm, he explained. But I declined the offer, even while assuring him that a bigger share in the firm was exactly what I wanted. Instead, I told him, I hoped to achieve that in a different way. I proposed we create a New Talent Division, which I would head. We'd make it our jobs to get back to what I loved doing most—traveling to high schools and colleges in the middle of nowhere, taking a chance on a kid no one had heard of. As it turned out, Alan loved the idea. Now that I was focusing on shaping and guiding the careers of our youngest clients, the work was less high-profile but infinitely more rewarding. I felt far more challenged creatively, thinking about how to make a young unknown into a household name, than I had been when I was simply fielding endorsement offers for the latest Super Bowl hero. Instead of thinking about short-term paydays, I was helping my newer clients map out long-term career goals. Pitching a young ice-hockey protégé or a budding gymnast was far trickier—riskier—and I certainly had my share of misses, but I'd also had some surprising successes. And I knew my old division was being well handled by our junior agents; it gave them a chance to stretch their abilities and grow into more senior roles.

I felt passionate about my work again. By becoming a mentor to the younger agents, I'd helped create an atmosphere of collaboration. As a pleasant by-product, business was booming.

Life outside the office had taken a turn for the better, too. I started to swim after work. I'd been dating a woman my age I met at the pool. I still travel to Montreal now and then, working with Diane and Cirque du Soleil to identify athletes who merit an audition.

Life was good.

Leading me deeper into the crowd that had gathered in the room, Diane said, "There's someone here tonight I'd like you to meet. She, too, has put in a lot of hard work and has overcome tremendous obstacles to get where she is today. She's a swimmer—the first you've met in your time at Cirque, if I'm not mistaken. But that's not all you two have in common; like you, Karine has seen how the choices she's made—and some of them weren't easy— have completely changed her life."

Curious, I followed Diane into the greenroom. A tall, beautiful woman with long, sandy-blond hair, wearing a summer dress walked toward us from backstage, holding a baby in her arms.

"This is Karine," Diane said. "And *this*," she added, leaning in to peek at the baby, "is Cherie. *Bonjour*, Cherie!"

Karine had grown up in Montreal, where, as a ten-year-old girl, she had idolized Romanian gold medalist Nadia Comaneci.

"I wanted to be a gymnast, but it became pretty obvious I was way too tall. I was a foot higher than the other girls my age! But I loved it, so I stuck with it.

"After our workouts, I would go to the pool for an hour

while I waited for my mom to pick me up. Because I was
tall and athletic, I could do laps pretty fast. One of the
coaches there saw me and asked me to join his team. At
first, it was great! I was winning races left and right. I even
left gymnastics behind. But after the thrill of the attention
wore off, swimming hundreds of laps, morning and night,
became a bit of a drag.

"Around the same time, I had started arriving a little
early for our evening practices to watch the synchronized
swimming team work out. It was fascinating. The sport was
just coming into its own then, and to me, it seemed like the
perfect combination of what I could do, swim, and what I
wanted to do, gymnastics. I soon joined the team.

"Speed swimming was work, but synchro practices were
fun! I liked the freedom. We were not restricted to a lane,
going back and forth like robots; we were making shapes,
spinning this way and pivoting that way, working together
to make something beautiful.

"I soon lost my desire to race. So I told my coach that I
was quitting the swimming club to join the synchro team.
He was stunned and heartbroken. It was so difficult for
me, because he had been such a good coach: tough but car-
ing. Everyone thought I was crazy. But sometimes you
have to make a leap like this.

"When I switched to synchro, I knew right away it was
the right thing for me. I wasn't great, but I loved it so
much, I got better fast. Within two years I was on the
national team, and by the time the '92 Olympics rolled
around, I was selected the solo swimmer on the team. One
day, I realized I needed to work on my stroke a bit for the

position they gave me, so I asked my old speed coach to help me. He had taught me how to swim, and he deserved to be there with me. He was this very intense man, but I could see the tears in his eyes! Mine, too.

"Getting ready for the '92 Olympics, my life seemed great. I was twenty-six, I had a chance to win a medal as the soloist for my country, and I was engaged to a well-known sports broadcaster. We were going to go to the Olympics together. We were the perfect couple!"

She paused to look at her tiny daughter with an odd, wistful look in her eyes. She finally looked up.

"Marc died suddenly a month before the Olympics," she said without flinching. "Now, I think we all have a choice, every day. And I had a choice about how I was going to respond. I was sad, devastated, destroyed—but I still had choices. A week after he died, I made a choice: *I am going to keep living. I am going to go to the Olympics.*"

I looked at Diane as Karine said this. I'd never told her anything about my friend Mike, and nothing in her eyes indicated that she knew how my own loss had prompted some of the decisions that had brought me to Cirque. Still, I suppose that after all her time at Cirque, she'd learned not only how to recognize lost souls but also exactly how to help us find ourselves again.

"I didn't care if I won anything," Karine said. "What mattered was that I was going to go. Somehow, I managed to pull myself together and win the gold medal. But even then, my trials were not yet over. Because of a judging error, the medal was taken away, and I had to wait for a year before it was awarded to me.

"But when I returned for the '96 Olympics, our team surprised people when we won the silver medal in the group competition. The only thing that counted as I stood on the podium was that I was with my teammates. I still belonged; I had not given up. It's because I went through challenges like these that I am who I am today."

She looked me directly in the eye when she said that, and then she looked down at her daughter.

"I learned something else at the Olympics," she said. "I really don't like competition that much. That's not the reason I was with my team every day. I like to be a part of a team, doing something active, something beautiful, something original.

"And that is why I wanted to join Cirque du Soleil. Our shows have nothing to do with being better than the person next to you. It's about finding the horizon and reaching for it. *That* is also why it has been so good, so natural, for me to go from being a swimmer to a coach—although I really think of myself as a teacher.

"There's a difference between wanting to compete and wanting to participate," she said. "There's a difference between being an athlete and being an artist. And now I'm learning about the difference between being a coach and being a teacher. To me, a coach is responsible for motivating the whole team. Well, I can do a motivational speech for a hundred people, but what I really love is the more intimate interactions. And that, to me, is teaching: one-on-one, working with someone on their technique, helping that person understand who he or she is.

"At Cirque, you have to touch the crowd every night.

To do that, you need to find the little pearl inside yourself and give it to the audience. When you are teaching someone, you help them find that pearl. And when I see them find it and share it with an audience, I feel I've achieved something.

"Think about how pearls are made—from a grain of sand, an irritant. Everything I like about myself today started with a grain of sand. Being too tall for gymnastics, switching to synchro, losing my fiancé. These were all difficult in their own way, but each time, I made a decision to go forward, to use them to make me better.

"We all have these grains of sand. But we need to nurture them, make them beautiful. For a time I worked with the twins in the double trapeze in 'O.' I told them, 'I do not want to see the trapeze. I want to see you. Just as I don't want to see the water when I see a synchronized swimmer, I don't want to see a hammer when I see beautiful cabinets, I don't want to see the palette when I look at a painting.' I want our artists to be weightless and free. And for that to happen, they need to find the pearl inside themselves.

"If you are an athlete, your coaches tell you 'do it my way'; the judges tell you if you're bad or good, according to what they think is right. That is not the way it works at Cirque—here, we tell you to be yourself. That's why I love my job. I'm involved with everyone, but I have individual time with each artist. I don't even think of it as work; it's a growing experience.

"Are we stressed? Yes! Do we complain sometimes? Of course! But do we love our jobs? Yes! We are paid to make people dream and fly and escape. Sometimes when I watch the show, I listen to the audience members, and when they leave the show, I ask them what they thought. If they say, 'Don't ask me now, it's too much'—that's the feeling we're all working to achieve.

"With Cirque there are rules, but from 7:30 to 9 and 10:30 to midnight our job is to touch people. I think it's rubbed off on my older daughter, Celeste. She used to be scared of makeup and costumes, until the Lizard in *Mystère* came up to us in the front row one night and whispered, 'Don't be scared,' and winked. And now she loves it! She loves Gerard, the clown usher, because he gets to throw the popcorn all over the place. She tells me, 'I'm going to have my own show, and I'm going to be a clown with a big pink nose.' At the dinner table she makes a teeterboard out of a fork and a spoon, and then does a rehearsal: '*Mesdames et messieurs*, ladies and gentlemen, welcome to Cirque du Soleil!'

"Most of our life we're put in a cage, where we sing the same song day in and day out. But life is not about being caged, life is about flying."

Giving Back

The next night, Cari made her debut in KÀ. As I walked into the grand theatre once again, I understood that my journey had finally come full circle. I'd traveled the world only to come back to the place I'd begun.

Cari was playing one of the archers who weave and climb through the audience before the show begins. She had been so thrilled to apply her swirly henna-like tattoos and don her costume. Because she'd be wearing a mask that covered the lower half of her face, I assumed I wouldn't be able to recognize her. But, scanning the warriors as they scaled the catwalks of the theatre, I could swear I saw one of them wink at me.

Backstage, after the show, Diane told me there was one last person she wanted me to meet. I followed Diane as she walked the long KÀ corridors to meet a slender, fit woman in a bright red suit. Diane introduced her as Monique and told me she was the contortion coach from "O."

"A pleasure," I said.

Diane asked Monique to explain how she'd come to Cirque. "In Mongolia," Monique began, in slightly halting English, "every family wants daughter to be in contortion. When girls are born, they test them right away for flexibility! Outside of soccer, it is only real international sport we have."

Diane interjected, "It's one of the few ways for a girl to get out of her village, which might have few modern utilities and conveniences."

"So many girls work hard to become contortionists," Monique said. "Every girl wants to be top. So I work very hard!

"Our coaches never yell. They don't need to. They can show you anger with just one eye! They start with children very young, and spend lot of time with us. Very encouraging, they bring us along with love.

"At nine years old, I know this is my future. At eleven I join circus, and public applauds.

"In circus I learn more, not about contortion, but about

performance. My coach tell me, you must never think it is just a trick. They want to see show, they want to see YOU, the artist."

"So how did you get to Cirque?" I asked.

"Very hard journey!" Monique said. "Mongolia is Communist. Cannot go very far. So when the Wall comes down, for us it's like dream. I join circus in Germany.

"Traditional circus in Mongolia, we never work with choreography. But in Cirque it is like theatre. I want to work like this, too. But I am getting old—thirty is old for contortion! I call Diane, they see me, they like me. I have to tell them truth. They cannot believe my age! But I show them what I do, and they say, 'Come!'

"I still perform some, but now I coach more. I learn so much at Cirque. Now I teach what I learn: dance, transitions, and movement are as important as contortion technique.

"So I live my dreams. I become better, too. Not just athlete now, but artist and coach. When you receive so much, like me, you want to give back. When you go to our shows, this is what you see: artists not just doing jobs, but giving back to audience. And audience knows this."

As we retraced our steps out of the coaches' office and through the theatre, I saw a small crowd gathering around a young girl warming up backstage. Diane told me the girl, Sofia, was the daughter of Manny, a musician in "O." Just seven, she was already learning contortion. Monique put a small boom box on the stage and pressed the play button. And Sofia very naturally began doing her thing, a combination of Mongolian contortion and Senegalese dance, entirely new to the world.

Sofia's dance was part tribal rite, part belly dance, and part gymnastics. She worked her way around the stage effortlessly, and eventually ended up on her stomach, seemingly poised for a push-up. Then she curled her legs all the way back over her shoulders; she could scratch her ear with her big toe if she wanted.

What caught my attention, though, was the warmth of her smile, and her liquid, expressive eyes. Rarely had I seen anyone more fully present, more completely alive.

I couldn't resist smiling and waving good-bye.

With her hands spread on the floor for balance, she waved back—with her right foot. And that, I realized, was Cirque's creative spirit, the creative spark that burns within us all; it was as innocent and powerful as the improvised wave of a little girl's foot.

Acknowledgments

In *The Spark*, the people at Cirque du Soleil talk about the importance of inspiration, collaboration, and trust to any creative endeavor. I can tell you the people involved in this book practiced what they preached.

I would first like to thank Roger Scholl, Editorial Director at Currency Doubleday, and Sarah Rainone, editor at Currency Doubleday, who first approached me and asked me to help write this book. The two of them fused the visions of a half-dozen people into a single, coherent story—an exercise akin to herding cats—and they both did so with aplomb and good cheer.

Lyn Heward created this book, choreographed my great adventure, and served as a guardian angel throughout my tour. It was her bold idea to give me the opportunity millions of Cirque fans would kill for, to become a member of the Cirque family for a few magical months. Rodney Landi, Cirque's master of merchandising, provided invaluable guidance and levity at crucial junctures, as did Marie-Josée Lamy, Cirque's director of licensing. Genevieve Bastien and Francine Tremblay were great allies, spending countless hours to make sure everything was just right. Louise Simoneau, Lyn Heward's longtime assistant, has served as den mother to thousands of Cirque faithful—including, for a few months, yours truly. Her generosity and warmth never failed. I cannot possibly thank the two-hundred-plus people who helped me along the way, but I will be sure to thank all of you when I see you again.

My writing friends James Tobin and John Lofy proved themselves once again to be great confidantes. Finally, I'd like to thank David Black, my uber-agent, and his assistant, David Larabell, for doing what they do better than anyone else: taking care of their writers.

I hope you enjoyed reading this tale as much as I enjoyed living it.

—John U. Bacon
Ann Arbor, Michigan, November 2005